LUKE 10
LEADERSHIP

"Wow, I really love this book! It's very readable and I found myself constantly highlighting ideas that resonated with my experience in parish life. Buy this book for your pastor, give a copy to a newly ordained priest or deacon, and share it with anyone discerning a leadership role in parish ministry. In four brief chapters, Fr. Dave Heney reveals a refreshing study of Luke 10 that will inspire parish leaders to authentically know, love, and evangelize God's people."

Sharon Ehrenkranz
Director of Parish Life
St. Laurence Catholic Church
Sugar Land, Texas

"*Luke 10 Leadership* should be required reading for everyone in Catholic ministry. Facing a culture that openly rejected the Christian way of life, increasingly similar to our world today, Jesus offered four simple things to do to transform hearts. In *Luke 10 Leadership*, Heney gives the reasons why these steps worked back then and why they can still work for Church leaders today."

Rich Curran
Executive Director
Parish Success Group

"What makes Fr. Dave Heney special is his insistence on being good at the mission and his intolerance for mediocrity. I don't know if I've ever met a pastor who's both so idealistic and so relentlessly practical at the same time."

From the foreword by **John L. Allen Jr.**
Editor of Crux

"Everyone in parish ministry needs this book. I will not be surprised if *Luke 10 Leadership* becomes required reading in lay, deaconal, and priestly formation because it carefully parses out best practices alongside Gospel principles. I wish I had this book as a guide when I first started in parish ministry! The lessons offered by Fr. Dave Heney will soften many of the hard-earned lessons encountered in parish ministry."

Roberto Chavez
Director of Faith Formation
Sacred Heart Parish, Colorado Springs, Colorado

LUKE 10
LEADERSHIP

How to Succeed at Parish Ministry

DAVE HENEY

AVE MARIA PRESS AVE Notre Dame, Indiana

Foreword © 2020 by John L. Allen Jr.

© 2020 by Dave Heney

Founded in 1865, Ave Maria Press is a ministry of the United States Province of Holy Cross.

www.avemariapress.com

Paperback: ISBN-13 978-1-59471-947-9

E-book: ISBN-13 978-1-59471-948-6

Cover illustration © Kat Chadwick/Getty Images.

Cover design by Andy Wagoner.

Text design by Brianna Dombo.

Printed and bound in the United States of America.

Library of Congress Cataloging-in-Publication Data
Names: Heney, Dave, 1952- author.
Title: Luke 10 leadership : how to succeed at parish ministry / Dave Heney.
Description: Notre Dame, Indiana : Ave Maria Press, 2020. | Summary: "Fr. Dave Heney shares his four-step; bible-based leadership plan that builds on four simple directives from Jesus found in Luke's gospel and shows readers how to: build trusting relationships, embrace the culture of their parish, tend to the wounded, and speak the Good News in ways that their people can understand"-- Provided by publisher.
Identifiers: LCCN 2019046023 (print) | LCCN 2019046024 (ebook) | ISBN 9781594719479 (paperback) | ISBN 9781594719486 (ebook)
Subjects: LCSH: Christian leadership--Catholic Church. | Pastoral theology--Catholic Church. | Church work--Catholic Church. | Parishes. | Bible. Luke, X--Criticism, interpretation, etc.
Classification: LCC BX1913 .H3675 2020 (print) | LCC BX1913 (ebook) | DDC 253/.32--dc23
LC record available at https://lccn.loc.gov/2019046023
LC ebook record available at https://lccn.loc.gov/2019046024

To all the parishioners in the parishes where I have served.
You have all taught me so much and I am grateful.

CONTENTS

FOREWORD BY JOHN L. ALLEN JR.

Fr. Dave Heney has written this book about effective parish leadership based on chapter ten of Luke's Gospel, but it's a different Bible passage with which I'm going to kick things off, Matthew 7:16: "By their fruits you will know them."

I've been privileged over the years to see the fruits of Fr. Dave's approach to parish leadership, and I can assure you, the guy knows what he's talking about. This isn't an abstract treatise written by someone sitting in a chancery office, or a graduate seminar; this is seasoned wisdom from the trenches, offered by a priest who's modeled genuinely effective parish leadership for decades.

Heney writes that this book is "designed to help you achieve the trust and confidence of your parishioners as you begin to lead them." I don't know if it'll actually do that—mostly, I suspect, that's up to you—but what I can report is that Heney has done it himself, over and over, under some truly trying circumstances.

I got to know Fr. Dave almost twenty years ago, when I was a young reporter in Rome struggling to explain the Vatican to the American media market and eager to round out my meager salary with some speaking gigs. Fr. Dave invited me to take part in his "University Series," a multi-parish adult education and faith formation program that rolls out during Lent, and so off I went.

I only have scattered memories of that long-ago first encounter—a good cigar and a stiff drink, great conversation over dinner (he seemed to know more about the Vatican than I did, and I get paid to cover the place), and a packed house in the parish. I remember thinking Heney was one of those dynamo priests you occasionally run into, an entrepreneur in a Roman collar who's always got a three-ring circus running someplace.

Over the years, those scattered first impressions have hardened into a permanent sense of amazement at Heney's energy and imagination. This is a pastor who just doesn't seem to have a middle gear. Even when I've thought he was off his rocker with a particular idea—and, believe me, he's had a couple doozies—I've always been impressed by the gusto with which he goes about it.

For two decades, I don't think I've ever had a conversation with Dave Heney in which he didn't light up talking about a new project, some new parish undertaking or media initiative or book manuscript or pilgrimage trip. Fundamentally, I came to understand that his drive isn't just about a strong work ethic or a gift for seizing market opportunities. He's an honest-to-God missionary, whose aim is to spread the Gospel and to bring souls to Christ, and who'll leave no stone unturned in that effort.

Lots of Catholics, of course, have the same missionary impulse. What makes Heney special is his insistence on being good at the mission, his intolerance for mediocrity. I don't know if I've ever met a pastor who's both so idealistic and so relentlessly practical at the same time.

Bear in mind, by the way, that Heney is a pastor in the Archdiocese of Los Angeles, arguably one of the places in the U.S. hardest hit by the clerical sexual abuse scandals in the Church. He lived through the explosion of 2002, the massive $660 million payout of 2007, and other cycles of revelations as time has gone on. Heney's no wide-eyed naïf, so he knows very well the massive damage the scandals have inflicted on the Church's public standing and on morale in the pews. Yet through it all, his energy has never flagged and his root optimism never dimmed, and sometimes I think his parishes have weathered the storm better than most simply by force of his personality.

As the years rolled on, I've kept up my annual appointment with the University Series, which is fairly unique on the Catholic landscape. I'm not aware of many other examples of a multi-parish program that's bottom-up, meaning not imposed by authority but created and sustained by the parishes themselves. By virtue of showing up every year, I've had the chance to spend time in and around parishes led by Heney, and I've noted several defining characteristics no matter where he's been.

First, there's a palpable sense of hustle. Heney's constantly asking the people around him what else can be done, which breeds a sense that the status quo is perennially open to question. He models a core principle of leadership – the trick isn't just doing things right, but finding the right things to do.

Second, there's a strong sense of lay empowerment. Most of the people I deal with on these occasions are laity inspired by Heney to lead, and it's clear they've taken ownership of the projects in which they're involved.

Third, there's a balanced approach to Church life, one not fractured along liberal/conservative lines but inspired by the "both/and" vision that Pope Benedict XVI once called the "genetic genius" of Catholicism.

Fourth, there's joy. Most people I've met over the years in a Fr. David Heney parish seemed to be having a blast, genuinely taking pleasure in the company of their pastor and one another.

Fifth, there's real curiosity and a lively sense of the life of the mind. People enjoy being informed, challenged, and even provoked. They tend to chew over ideas and generally aren't content with bland, cookie-cutter answers. In that way, too, they tend to reflect the personality of their pastor.

I wish I could tell you that I know how to bottle and sell all that, but I don't. To be honest, I'm not really convinced you can "learn" effective leadership at all. Sometimes I suspect it's one of those innate qualities that people are either born with or not, and everything else is just refinement and gloss.

What I do know, however, is this: If a book can help you become a more effective parish leader, this is the right one. And if the key to such a book is finding the right author, then you're in good hands with Fr. Dave Heney.

As we'd say here in Rome, *Buona lettura*!

ACKNOWLEDGMENTS

I am especially grateful to a few people who have been immensely helpful during this book project.

After finishing a twelve-year term as pastor at St. Paschal Baylon Parish in Thousand Oaks, California, and my home parish, I began a sabbatical research year to prepare this book. I thank Archbishop Gomez who allowed for this special opportunity.

I was also granted a visiting research fellowship with the Nicola Center for Ethics and Culture at the University of Notre Dame. I am grateful to its director, Carter Snead, for his friendship and enthusiasm for this project. I am proud to have been associated with this outstanding Catholic intellectual and pastoral resource.

I am grateful, as always to Paul and Marsha Griffin, for their friendship and support over many years, and making office space available to me during the sabbatical year spent in California.

To Ed and Lynn Hogan, and their son, Glenn, for their amazing hospitality when I stayed at their beautiful St. Francis Ranch to continue my studies. Their example of faith and generosity were deeply inspirational to me during my research.

I add my gratitude for my classmate, Fr. Joseph Shea, for his hospitality during this book-writing time.

Finally, I am grateful to John Allen, the most trusted commentator on Catholic Church affairs today, for his friendship and support for many years, and for writing the foreword to this book.

Of course, I am deeply honored to be associated with Ave Maria Press, the premier pastoral publishing company in the United States today. I am grateful to Eileen Ponder, who shepherded this project from the beginning, and always had helpful advice. She is part of a remarkable team of publishing professionals who only desire to make helpful materials available to parish ministers today.

I have drawn on the experiences of many parishes since my ordination in 1978. All of them have been enormously helpful in gaining insights into Our Lord's plan for pastoral ministry among his people. I hope they will find just the support they need as each parish continues to make the person of Jesus Christ present and alive among their people today.

INTRODUCTION

After this, the Lord appointed seventy-two
others whom he sent ahead of him in pairs to
every town and place he intended to visit.

—Luke 10:1

I expect you are reading this book as a newly appointed pastor,
newly ordained priest or deacon, recently hired catechetical or faith
formation leader, a youth minister, new pastoral council member,
or another leader beginning a new role in your Catholic parish.
You may feel hesitant, anxious, or perhaps even fearful about your
new responsibilities. Well, Jesus has some wonderful advice about
leadership just for you! At the beginning of chapter 10 in the Gospel
of Luke, Jesus sends out seventy-two disciples and the instructions he gives them remain just what today's Church leaders still
need. I wrote this book to make our Lord's ideas easy to understand
and put into practice so that your ministry will be as effective and
rewarding as he wants it to be for you and for the community you
serve.

Luke's gospel provides us a detailed description of the saving
message, life, death, and Resurrection of Jesus. By the time he was
writing, several decades after the death of Jesus, some people were
already distorting what Jesus said and did, so Luke set out to correct the distortions by writing an accurate and orderly account
(see Luke 1:1–4). He wisely consulted eyewitnesses to make sure
he had the story right, and his careful detective work produced,
in Luke 10:5–9, a record of Jesus' instructions for evangelization,
which are, perhaps surprisingly, extremely helpful for those of us
called to leadership in the Church today.

Some two thousand years later, we live in circumstances quite similar to those that Luke faced. The message of Jesus has been distorted in many ways throughout our often-turbulent history as a church and as a culture. False claims about what Jesus taught are often made. Not for the first time, the Church now faces terrible scandal and a painful crisis in leadership, both of which make stepping into a new role more complicated for you than it might otherwise be. Priests have lost much of the automatic respect we enjoyed for years as pillars not only of the Church but of our wider communities. Deacons and lay ministers are not always welcomed in parishes as legitimate leaders or authorities in their areas of responsibility.

Parishioners today who are well educated, carefully trained professionals in a wide variety of fields frequently lament the lack of professional expertise they see in some priests and parish ministers who have never, or perhaps only minimally, trained in organizational leadership. They are right to do so. While many lay professionals are required to update their skills with continuing education, very few dioceses *require* such seminars for clergy and lay ministers. In fact, too many dioceses place people in leadership positions without much attention to their competence in leading people or overseeing the complex organizational structures a parish ought to have. While these assignments may be well intentioned, they can set up a sincere and well-meaning new pastor, associate pastor, deacon, or lay parish minister for failure and tragically disillusion them for the future. That should never happen.

HOW THIS BOOK CAN HELP

You may already have extensive experience in leading organizations, either in the Church or perhaps in the business world. Experience can certainly provide confidence that you are ready for leadership. Yet ironically, the sign that you are truly experienced is a hunger to learn even more. The most effective leaders always feel the tug of further growth, even in areas where they have worked for years. They *continuously* improve pertinent skills. Jesus must have been amused at his disciples, who quickly assumed titles of "Rabbi" (teacher) and "Master" (Mt 23:8, 10). It probably never occurred to them that they were arrogant. Make sure you are not. Instead of thinking of ourselves as teachers, Jesus proposes that we in leadership consider ourselves learners. Many of his teachings begin with words such as *seek, find,* or *ask.* Jesus even calls himself "meek and humble of heart" (Mt 11:29). Let us seek leadership in that same humble way so that no one will ever say that we acted like Pharisees . . . or arrogant disciples. Consider Peter, whose sometimes-overinflated ego and failures did not keep Jesus from naming him to lead the Church. He certainly had a steep learning curve and must have been embarrassed, probably even chagrined, at hearing stories of his early days as a companion of Jesus repeated time and again when early Christians gathered for Eucharist. Everyone knew that Peter's behavior back then was really not the best! But Peter learned humility and accepted his role in leadership.

A special burden that all Church leaders, whether clergy or laity, carry today is the horrible legacy of the abuse scandals that have so traumatized our parishioners. Parishioners may understandably be suspicious of any new leader who arrives at their parish. You were, no doubt, googled the instant you were announced as a parish leader. You are under more scrutiny today than ever before. You can be sure parents will want to know quickly if you are a person whom they can trust with their children. Your integrity is immediately in question.

You arrive with a handicap not of your making, your good name and reputation at stake right away. Such was also the case at the time of the early Church. Christians were outliers in Roman culture, following a religion that was suspect because it was new and not in accord with Roman pagan beliefs and practices. Jesus prepared his disciples specifically for the difficulties and resistance they were sure to meet, so perhaps you can feel a connection with that heroic first generation of leaders who faced deep suspicion and even persecution.

Fortunately, most people truly want to feel proud of our Church and its leaders again. They will be reassured by the clear way you address any issue the Church faces. I hope these short chapters will provide a clear path to help you find success and happiness in your ministry. They are designed to help you achieve the trust and confidence of your parishioners as you begin to lead them. Most importantly, they arise from the very teachings of Jesus right there in the opening verses of Luke 10.

Despite the many challenges, the first disciples successfully led Christian communities with optimism and confidence in the midst of a hostile pagan culture. They were trained by our Lord and trusted that his way of introducing the kingdom of God would work—and we know it can work today as well. This book will guide you through what I call our Lord's "Luke 10 Leadership" training for pastors, priests, deacons, and lay ministers to lead Catholic parishes today with that same optimism and confidence.

LUKE 10 LEADERSHIP

At the end of the ninth chapter of Luke, Jesus resolves to travel to Jerusalem through the hostile territory of Samaria, sending advance teams of his disciples ahead of him to prepare the way. That was a courageous choice. There were other, safer ways to travel to Jerusalem, such as along the Jordan River Valley to the east, yet Jesus opted to go directly through an unfriendly area, sending his disciples right into hostile territory. His disciples must have wondered and likely worried about how this journey would turn out. They knew that Samaritans practiced a form of Judaism that caused friction with the mainline Jews of Jerusalem and Galilee and that most Jews avoided Samaria and Samaritans. In the same manner, Samaritans would never associate with Jews like Jesus and his followers. Samaria also included Greco-Roman villages filled with people who thought of Jews as alien and opposed to their own culture. A lot of tension there!

It's not hard to understand, then, that Samaritans, Greeks, and Romans viewed Jesus and his followers with suspicion. Yet Jesus boldly decided to go precisely to places filled with tensions, presumably knowing full well that he and his followers would not be met with a friendly reception. He planned his approach wisely and carefully. Fortunately for us, Luke records in the beginning of chapter 10 the important advice Jesus gave his disciples as he sent them ahead to make ready for his arrival. Jesus advised his followers to act among the Samaritans the same way he directed them to act in every place they traveled for the rest of their years as disciples.

JESUS' WISE AND CAREFUL PLAN FOR EVANGELIZATION

During the first century, before the gospels and letters of the New Testament were even written, no one was under more suspicion than our own heroic ancestors in faith. They were a small band of disciples living within the immense Roman Empire, which was then about the same size as the continental United States. It encompassed most of modern Europe, North Africa, and the Middle East, with colonies from the far north of England to western Spain and east to modern-day Syria and Iraq. Moreover, none of the inhabitants of this vast empire believed as the disciples believed that Jesus had come as savior. They were alone in this.

So how were they to reach the people they encountered? What approach would work? In ancient times, the expected way to try to change a foreign culture was to conquer it with military force. Well, the disciples had no army and no weapons; worse still, they were led by former fishermen! How could they possibly succeed? Jesus could see how, and he had a plan.

Jesus' vision of and plan for leadership centered entirely on the behavior and example of his followers. After all, the early community of his followers had no buildings—no church halls, no cathedrals. They had no websites, radio, or television stations; no social media platforms; no schools, colleges, hospitals, or universities. They certainly had no army! They did not even have the New Testament scriptures yet. They were only people, and fairly simple people at that. Jesus' plan for evangelization and leadership, outlined in Luke 10:5–9, would be built on what ordinary people could do.

Jesus said to them, "The harvest is abundant but the laborers are few; so ask the master of the harvest to send out laborers for his harvest" (Lk 10:2). Notice that Jesus did not ask for *more* laborers; he asked that the laborers he already had would respond well to his instruction to go out and reap the harvest. That was a remarkable expression of confidence in his very small band of followers and is a reminder of the confidence that our Lord has in you.

The seventy-two disciples of Luke 10 listened closely to Jesus as he sent them out. They knew they had a powerful message of salvation to offer people in those difficult places; but Jesus knew that even the goodness of his message was never enough! Our Lord's plan went beyond just speaking beautiful words of salvation. He asked for more from those he sent out, and he asks for more from you. How often do we assume that because we have a solid, true, and authentic message to give, all we have to do is simply announce it and people will follow? Well, they very well may not follow, for many good reasons which include our own lack of being well trained and prepared for leadership. Hopefully this little book will help to remedy that.

PREPARING THE GROUND ACCORDING TO LUKE 10

The parable of the sower is instructive here. Take a few minutes to read it (see Luke 8:4–15). The farmer in this story has excellent seed to sow in a field, but he *haphazardly* throws the seed all over the place: some lands on rocky ground, some on hard ground, and some even among thorns. Farmers then would never do that! Good seed is too valuable. A wise farmer first carefully prepares the ground so that every seed will take root and a great harvest will grow. Jesus calls his disciples to be like that wise farmer who carefully prepares the ground, so that their every evangelizing action will produce a good harvest.

Jesus himself instructed the earliest disciples on how to be successful and effective ministers; we should carefully heed that lesson. Knowing his disciples well and deeply understanding how human beings behave, Jesus devised a model of leadership that still proves both effective for announcing the kingdom of God and profoundly rewarding for you as a leader.

Luke 10 offers a number of helpful instructions on Christian leadership and evangelization; these four main steps are the focus of this book:

1. "Into whatever house you enter, **first say, 'Peace to this household'**" (v. 5).
2. "Whatever town you enter and they welcome you, **eat what is set before you**" (v. 8).
3. "**[C]ure the sick**" (v. 9).
4. "**[S]ay to them, 'The kingdom of God is at hand for you'**" (v. 9).

The next four chapters will delve into what these instructions meant to Jesus' disciples in the first-century Roman Empire and what they mean for you today.

1.
FIRST SAY PEACE

"Go on your way; behold, I am sending you
like lambs among wolves. Carry no money bag,
no sack, no sandals; and greet no one along the
way. Into whatever house you enter, first say,
'Peace to this household.' If a peaceful person
lives there, your peace will rest on him; but if
not, it will return to you."

—Luke 10:3–6

KEY IDEAS

Jesus sent his disciples into a hostile Roman culture and sends you now into a world that has grown at least suspicious of, if not openly hostile toward, institutional religion. Jesus says you must first say peace because it is not enough to simply be at peace. You have to say and visibly signal by your behavior that you mean no harm. And you need to do that right up front! The angels at Bethlehem said this peace right away at our Lord's birth, when people would have expected the Messiah to arrive with an avenging army for all their sinfulness. That proactive signaling of peace is especially important in cross-cultural ministry, where you might lead a community that has experienced hostility and discrimination.

There are many ways to say peace. Your dress, your behavior, and—most important—your facial expression are all opportunities to say peace. Your parish buildings, office procedures, communications, and staff behaviors can also say peace. Finally, the manner in which you handle problems, particularly conflicts with parishioners, is a powerful way to demonstrate your commitment to first communicating peace (that you intend no harm).

Jesus started his instructions by directing his disciples to first say peace. First words are important. The seventy-two would have paid close attention to what Jesus said first in preparing them to lead as his disciples, especially since they knew what suspicion and resistance they would meet where they were headed! Jesus let them know that it was not enough for them simply to *be* at peace with people they met; as his disciples, they must *say* peace. They must visibly and audibly signal peace up front, before any other interaction or conversation took place.

THE IMPORTANCE OF SAYING PEACE IN THE ROMAN EMPIRE

Why was that so important? Jesus was sending them into clearly hostile Greco-Roman and Samaritan territory. Because they were going among people who already had a negative opinion of them, they had to convey proactively that they meant no harm, had come in peace, and respected the people of the places where Jesus sent them.

There is a lot of new scholarly interest in this time of Church history and in how these former fishermen were so successful. Understanding the cultural context of our early-Church ancestors and the challenges they faced reveals the wisdom of the instructions our Lord gave to his disciples then—and gives to us today. Let's take a closer look at this ancient world in which our Lord founded his Church. You will be amazed at how courageous our spiritual

ancestors were to leave familiar surroundings and go among enemies. Here is what they were up against.

Samaritan Suspicion

Some of the people living in Samaria, the area south of Galilee
where the disciples were sent, were Jewish people who had inter-
married with pagans and developed a hybrid form of Judaism and
so were no longer considered truly Jewish by mainstream Judaism.
Orthodox Jewish people like Jesus and his disciples would normally
never travel through Samaria. Obviously, Samaritans would not
look kindly on Jewish emissaries from Jesus either . . . yet here
they were!

Roman Paranoia

Several centuries before Christ, Rome was conquered by Gallic
armies from what is now France. This trauma caused the Roman
people to embark on centuries of conquest. By conquering neigh-
boring tribes, they extended the boundary of Roman territory farther and farther from the city of Rome itself, thus better ensuring
their safety. A deep fear of any repeat of that earlier humiliating
Gallic conquest drove the vastness of Roman conquest. The Romans
feared even the smallest threat from any of their conquered peoples.
Although it seems counterintuitive, the mighty Roman Empire
actually rested on fragile egos, profound fears, and deep suspicions.
    Roman religion addressed these fears with a mechanism for
avoiding evil and ensuring safety, but the Roman religious sense
was very different from our Christian sensibilities today. The many
Roman gods were emotionally distant figures who acted very much
like tyrants. They expected sacrifices and offerings of incense in
payment for their protection from disaster or bestowal of blessings.
Roman religion was actually a form of extortion.
    Humans did not have personal relationships with the gods
of any of the ancient religions—Greek, Assyrian, Babylonian, or

Egyptian. It was all transactional. If you sacrificed a goat or the first fruits of a harvest, you might receive protection from sickness, victory in battle, or an abundant harvest. Nothing was asked of you morally: just pay the sacrifice, and you were in good standing. Therefore, Roman authorities made sure that every citizen paid the gods to ensure their protection and blessings for the empire.

The followers of Jesus and the strange codes they lived by were seen as great threats to Roman safety and security. Five specific early Christian behaviors and beliefs, which Luke would have known well when he told the story of Jesus sending out the seventy-two, made Roman authorities particularly nervous.

- *The followers of Jesus did not offer sacrifice to the Roman gods.*
  Romans saw those who followed Jesus as treasonous and a drain on the empire. For example, if there was a bad harvest or an enemy threatening Rome, it was easy to blame Christians for angering the gods by failing to make sacrificial offerings to the gods, and especially to the emperor. By the time of Luke's writing, even living Roman emperors were often declared gods and they expected to be worshipped. This was as a sign of civic obedience. Yet, Christians would never accept a Roman emperor as a god. When Romans would say, "Caesar is Lord," Christians would emphatically respond with, "No, Jesus is Lord!"

- *Christians met in small groups frequently.* Roman leaders were deeply suspicious of any hint of subversion, which often begins in small gatherings. They therefore outlawed unapproved private meetings of groups of ten or more. Yet meeting is exactly what Christians did every Sunday, and sometimes even during the week.

- *Christian groups included people from all levels of society.* In the ancient world, people belonged to clearly defined social classes: land owners, important patrons, politicians, military leaders, peasants, and—at the bottom of the social ladder—slaves. In that world, you only mixed with people from your own level. People of the Roman Empire were suspicious of Christian worship, where people of different classes gathered together in fellowship. Rich, poor, men, women, soldiers, and slaves all together!? There had to be some ill intent among them.

- *The followers of Jesus took care of anyone who was sick.* In the ancient world, your own family was your *only* concern, and you would feel and do little for your neighbors next door. Most people assumed sickness was caused by the gods' disfavor; therefore, the sick were avoided and even abandoned. Better to side with the gods than with those they disfavored! With that lack of care, the sick often died quickly. Romans were perplexed by the disciples of Jesus, who cared for the sick—amazingly even those outside their own families. Ironically, the Christian practice of caring for anyone in need that they could help, led to some people being cured, which the Romans noticed, leading to further suspicions about Christian practices. It also slowly increased their curiosity about the Christian response of love to those who are sick and the dramatic power of that love to heal.

- *Jesus taught that God loved all people.* In a world where religion was a purely transactional relationship of sacrifices in exchange for favors, Romans were perplexed at the concept of a Christian God who actually *loved* them *unconditionally* and did not extort sacrifices for protection or blessings. Roman gods didn't act like that!

Roman vigilance against threats was constant. Across the ancient world, revenge was required for every perceived attack, and each of these behaviors and beliefs, common among the followers of Jesus, would likely have been perceived as an attack on Roman culture. Jesus understood this and yet still sent his disciples forward. It's easy to see his wisdom in telling them to speak peace first, to signal that they meant no harm.

JESUS SAID PEACE FROM THE BEGINNING

The angels who announce Jesus' birth to shepherds in the second chapter of Luke's gospel tell their hearers not to be afraid and speak peace to those on whom God's favor rests (see Luke 2:8–14). Jesus is born into a world of violence and sin, but he does not arrive as a warrior ready for battle, nor with an army, nor as a god to bring vengeance on a sinful people. Rather, Jesus comes as a poor, vulnerable child without a home—hardly a threat to anyone! This is an amazing demonstration of how our Lord engages those he has come to serve and to save. He comes in peace, a message first spoken by the angels. This is how he wants us, as leaders of his Church, to engage our world too; Jesus now sends you in peace just as he came in peace.

Jesus' meek arrival in Bethlehem and the message of peace announced by the angels were important signs for those seventy-two disciples in Luke 10. Jesus knew he was sending them into a world weary of hatred and violence yet filled with resentment and a thirst for revenge. And so he knew it would be crucial for his disciples to present themselves immediately as nonthreatening, seeking no harm to those they met. He wanted them to appear as humble as a newborn child. He thus instructed his disciples to first say peace.

This is great guidance for those of us called to Church leadership today. It is not just a clever ploy or sales technique. Jesus truly means for us to greet people in peace just as he came in peace at Bethlehem, showing them that we are leaders who truly and deeply mean no harm. This peaceful stance cannot be faked or simulated; people will very quickly catch on if it is, which in itself brings harm. Saying peace first, before we do anything else, means we value the other person as one created by God and possessing inherent dignity—no matter whether they are friend or foe. We express by our words and actions that we wish them well and want to know them, even before we know whether they will accept us or not!

Why does Jesus place this step first? Because he knows our human nature better than anyone. He knows how to connect with people, no matter who they are.

THE CONFIDENCE OF
"I AM WITH YOU ALWAYS"

It takes profound confidence and courage to first say peace in an uncertain environment. The gospels tell stories of Jesus working miracles in one town, where the reaction is praise, and then doing the same in the next town and being accused of blasphemy. Yet in each village he was serenely the same. His head did not get big with praise, nor did he collapse in depression with rejection. How was that possible? It could only be because our Lord was deeply connected to his Father in heaven and sought only to follow his will. Jesus' sense of self, as psychologists might call it today, did not depend on the acclaim or the disdain of others, but only on loving his Father in heaven.

During his ministry, Jesus seemed not to feel alone. It is the feeling of being alone or isolated that allows fear to enter in. When accompanied by close friends and trusted allies, we feel we can face anything. Our Lord is our friend and trusted ally in parish leadership at every moment of every day. There is never any need to feel fear.

Jesus offered his disciples this supremely empowering idea to provide strength and stability no matter where they found themselves. In fact, Jesus' final words in Matthew's gospel are "I am with you always, until the end of the age" (28:20). This means that we do not have to hope that we meet only nice people each day in order for us to be okay. With our Lord at our side, we are always okay no matter whom we meet.

This in turn means that our behavior will not be determined by the actions of other people. Jesus changes the ancient culture of revenge—summarized as "If you treat me well, I will treat you well;

if you treat me badly, I will hurt you terribly!"—to "If you treat me well, I will treat you well; if you treat me badly . . . I will treat you well!" As parish leaders, we can freely choose at the start of each day to follow Jesus and determine just how we will act, no matter whom we meet later on and no matter how they treat us. We choose to follow the example of our Lord no matter what other people do. This is enormously empowering!

Jesus knew his disciples would be meeting all kinds of people, many of whom would be challenging characters. Most would be skeptics; some would perhaps be selfish, mean-spirited, or even violent people. He taught his disciples, and is teaching us today, to be self-possessed, abiding in his presence and mastering our own behavior, even in the face of adversity.

Never Let Another Person's Lack of Faith, Hope, or Love Affect Yours!

As you begin your new role in leadership, you can expect to encounter people much like those our heroic ancestors in the faith encountered as they set out to spread the message of Jesus. You can face whatever difficulties you encounter in much the same way that Jesus taught the seventy-two he sent out in the opening of Luke 10. He instilled in all his followers—our ancestors in faith—the gifts of faith, hope, and love and encouraged them to nourish and protect those precious virtues that will keep you steady and secure no matter what you might encounter.

How do we say peace? There are many ways, both personal and institutional.

INTRODUCE YOURSELF TO YOUR PARISH

St. Paul was most famous for writing letters to churches he had already visited, often in order to correct problems or answer questions about past events. However, Paul wrote an extensive theological introduction of himself, which we now have as the Letter to the Romans, *before* he travelled to Rome. He knew the importance of making himself known before he arrived.

Before you start a new parish position, you might think about mimicking Paul's approach. How can you make your values, principles, hopes, and dreams known to your people before you even arrive? All of your first events in your new parish should have that agenda—making yourself known. Be appropriately vulnerable, and let people get to know you—what you think, value, and hope for—just as Jesus was immediately heralded in Bethlehem and as Paul made himself known in Rome.

Vulnerability and Cross-Cultural Ministry

Beginning a new position with a willing vulnerability is especially important in parishes with large minority populations. Their lives have been lived within another, more dominant culture than their own, whether here in the United States or in their countries of origin, and many have grown suspicious or wary of those in positions of authority. They may have an overt, or more often unconscious, suspicion of any new leader coming to their parish. Members of ethnic or other minorities may be accustomed to keeping their opinions to themselves—often a safer course under authoritarian domination. Therefore, immediately asking minority staff members probing questions about parish operations may not work out well. Your up-front disclosure about who you are and your enthusiasm to be there for them can help alleviate suspicions. Those who live on the fringes of our neighborhoods, cities, and country often have a quite intense need to see and understand you first before they will disclose much of anything about themselves. Respect this, and remember to first say peace.

Never Make People Guess How You Feel about Them!

As a parish authority figure, whether clergy or a layperson, you have a role that people may respond to in unexpected ways because of circumstances or experiences that have nothing to do with you and that those people may not even be aware of. You are now a boss or an authority figure, and that means some people may relate to you with skepticism or even suspicion because of negative history with authority figures. You can help by indicating your peaceful intentions toward them up front and right away. At first meeting, you can quickly dispel and displace hesitancies with an accurate communication of your peaceful intentions and then follow up with continued efforts to communicate peace.

There will also be individuals who assume toward you what feels to you like a too-intimate posture. These individuals may have had a very close friendship with the person who previously filled your role. This can be awkward and quickly lead to misunderstandings. You will want to indicate appropriate boundaries. Even so, it's important to find ways to communicate that you come in peace, with good intentions, and seek a good relationship that will benefit the parish as well as both of you.

When you walk into a meeting, parish event, or any circumstance at all, you will normally not know how others are feeling. They also will not know how you are feeling. You can set the emotional tone right away with your first comments and, of course, your facial expression. Don't forget to smile! Jesus taught his followers to proactively set the tone for each encounter, every meeting along the way, with a gesture of peace and welcome, so be the first to greet people warmly, no matter who they are or how they might present themselves to you.

The Halo Effect

The "halo effect" is a well-known dynamic. It means that in the absence of information about someone, we will attribute our own biased information to them according to our already-determined feelings about them. For example, if a close friend whom you admire is late for a meeting, you will probably ascribe only good motives. You may think or say to the group, "My friend must be helping someone in need." You have, in effect, given your friend a halo or an aura of beneficence. You have interpreted his or her tardiness in a quite charitable light. However, if you do not like the person who is late for your meeting, you might well think more along the lines of "Once again, this idiot is forgetful, selfish, and rude!"

Jesus instructed the seventy-two and directs us today to make sure that people know from the first moment of an encounter that we come in peace. If you can live by this simple rule, you will find very soon that others will rarely, if ever, assert the worst interpretations of your behavior.

YOUR FACE MUST SIGNAL PEACE

One of the most meaningful ways of saying peace is through our face. Never underestimate that! It is not a small thing by any means. Our million-year history of evolution affirms it.

Those of us who are sighted are attuned first to the faces of people we meet . . . just as they are attuned to ours. God designed us to have amazing powers of facial interpretation. We can read even the smallest facial expressions to predict the intentions of those we are looking at. By observing that the white areas of a person's eyes are more on one side of their pupils than the other, we can tell even from a hundred feet away whether a person is looking directly at us or at the person next to us. We may miss every other detail in the room, and we often do, but not often will we miss where a person is looking. Evolution over millions of years has selected for this amazing human capacity.

Our ability to read other human faces also facilitates a crucial function of human interactions—making some judgment or determination about "what that person over there is thinking or, more importantly, expecting of me." Psychologists call this critical human mental capacity "theory of mind," and it represents our highest, most sophisticated, and most robust mental activity. Through brain-scanning technology, scientists today know that we exhibit the highest brain nerve cell activity when we try to ascertain what someone else is thinking. This capacity of ours is one of the main causes of our evolutionary success as a species.

Years ago, after moving to a new parish, I found myself in a store getting things I needed for my new office. Somewhat bored, I wandered the aisles absentmindedly, eventually coming across a display of office security cameras that had a monitor hooked up to a live camera. Gradually I recognized that I was looking at my own face on that screen, and I was horrified! My unsmiling, rather bored face actually looked somewhat mean! Hopefully, none of my new parishioners saw me that day, but if any did, I would understand if they had been reluctant to say hello after seeing my face.

If you ever wonder why people react to you the way they do, you should, at the very least, ponder the possibility that it might be the expression you innocently and inadvertently present. There is an old saying that hands move things, but faces move people. Never underestimate the power of your face as the first communicator of who you are. Please make sure it communicates that you come to do no harm, that you come in peace.

TREAT YOUR FELLOW TEAM MEMBERS WELL

The CEO of a large company once asked the members of his senior staff if they knew the names of any of the building's custodial staff.

He wanted to know if they ever talked with the people who kept the break room and restrooms clean and well stocked and vacuumed their offices at the end of each day. Few did. The CEO admonished his team to think again, could they at least picture faces? Would they recognize the custodians outside the office? He then pointed out that each and every person was important and valued in the company. Each person contributed to the company's success and ought to be treated with dignity, beginning with being called by name and acknowledged as an important coworker. Wise advice!

Jesus knew that people would notice the behavior *between* his disciples and would see if their behavior was genuine. That is why he sent his disciples out in pairs. After all, if you cannot express love for your fellow disciples, why should people follow you? Parishioners see right away if your behavior is authentic when they see how you relate and interact with people on your team. Words are cheap. Behavior is everything. Treat your fellow team members well whether you are a paid staff member or a volunteer leader in your parish. Respect each member of your leadership staff, ministry team, or leadership group, and always be sure your interactions show that you do. Learn to know the strengths and gifts of these others as well as you know your own, and be mindful always that your team together is a model of shared ministry and dynamic discipleship—indeed a living sign of Christ present in his Church.

The followers of Jesus valued every person, no matter what their social status or to what family they belonged. This surely would have puzzled many Romans, whose cultural norms held power, prestige, and one's own family in higher esteem than everything else. Social status meant everything. One of the first reactions Romans had about Jesus' followers was a very beautiful one recorded by the second-century theologian Tertullian: "Look, how they love one another and are ready to die for each other!"

Whenever parishioners see you with fellow staffers, they will take notice. This is especially true for priests in the same parish. Always think about how you appear in public together and what your behavior reveals about your relationship with each other. If you have any criticism of your fellow priests or staffers, be sure to express it privately, never in public. Even if you reconcile later after a public spat, the image of that public fight will live on for a long time in destructive parish gossip and rumors.

The Power of Two

Jesus sent *only two* disciples to each village . . . not more! Jesus somehow felt that two were enough. He had that much confidence in the power of two people to make a difference. Never underestimate that power.

Years ago, I was privileged to meet St. Teresa of Calcutta at an outdoor Mass in Tijuana, Mexico. I was understandably nervous about meeting her and so had practiced a thousand times my simple opening comment, "Good morning, Mother Teresa. It is nice to meet you!" I practiced it over and over again to make sure I would get it right. After all, how many times was I likely to meet a woman of such enormous significance on the world stage and such profound holiness? Finally, I was there at the Mass site—when *she* walked up to *me*. She immediately greeted me with a smiling face and said, "Welcome, Father. Are you from around here, or up in Los Angeles?" I said, "Los Angeles." She said, "Well, it is very hot today. I hope you have the chance to go to the beach later on. Thank you for coming!" I then said, "No problem!" Then I thought . . . did I just say "No problem!" to Mother Teresa?

Well, I never got to say my well-practiced phrase, simple as it was, but I was struck by how normal and natural her conversation was, and how her first concern was my comfort on a hot day. She said peace in the exact manner that our Lord describes in Luke 10. She did not expect or wait for me to enter her world, but rather she entered my experience of being in a very hot place and expressed her concern about that—about *me* on a very hot day. What a profoundly simple and crucial lesson for us who are leaders, not on the world stage, but in our parish communities.

PERSONAL ATTRIBUTES AND PRACTICES THAT FIRST SAY PEACE

We have looked at the power of your face to impact people and the transformative value of the example you set by how you interact with others. A welcoming expression and respectful behavior are fundamental characteristics of successful Church leaders. They go a long way in conveying your genuine love for people and are great methods of saying peace before you do anything else.

Your physical appearance is another way you can first say peace. This includes how you dress, your manners and etiquette, and your bearing or demeanor. These may seem like old-fashioned ideas, but never underestimate their power to affect the first impression others have of you.

Because you are a public leader in your parish, many eyes will be on you in any gathering. People will look to see how you conduct yourself in various social settings much more than they will watch anyone else. Rather than view getting to know the people in your new parish in a negative light—as though you are somehow on trial—think of these occasions as great opportunities to showcase your polite, considerate, welcoming behavior that others may even admire. Why not use the reality that people notice you for the good of your mission? After all, would you rather be ignored? I hope not! Getting attention for how you look and interact with others is a helpful tool and great gift for your ministry. Use it wisely!

We cannot . . . *not* communicate! *Everything* we do or say expresses something. Taking the time to reflect on the many ways you actually communicate is a useful and important pastoral exercise. Here are some additional ways you can first say peace in your parish.

Be Respectful in Your Clothing, Manners, and Bearing

Long before people see your facial expressions or hear you talk, they see how you are dressed. Your clothing always "speaks" something about you. What is it that you want to say through your clothes? Consider what your choice of clothing says. Neatness, cleanliness, and clothing are signs of respect that you communicate to your people. If you are clergy, you might want to consider when and where you wear your collar, why, and what message you want to convey.

If you are invited to a parishioner's home for dinner, you should assume it is an important opportunity for ministry and also anticipate an enjoyable event. People will observe how you conduct yourself, especially your table manners. Review how to introduce one person to another easily. Practice good conversational techniques, and make sure not to interrupt people or dominate discussions. Reading a good book on simple etiquette is a great investment of your time! It will pay you back many times over by helping you develop a good reputation in your parish. You should see these social events not as burdens at all but rather as wonderful opportunities to first say peace and easy ways to communicate respect and honor for your people.

Bearing is admittedly an old-fashioned word, but nevertheless a powerful one. It simply means how you stand or carry yourself. Are you hunched over or slumped in a chair? Do you convey a sense of confidence in the way you walk and move? Latest research indicates that changing your posture can also change your mood: people can feel more confident when they stand in a confident manner. Your body communicates all the time. It is worth paying attention to how you sit, stand, and walk. People notice. Regular exercise, including stretching, will help with your posture and your manner of walking. A quick internet search can lead you to simple exercises to help you get started if you aren't already established in a fitness routine.

Be Visible

Visibility is certainly a priority for communicating that you come in peace, seeking the good of all. It means that you are present at as many parish events as you can be, in the front where people can see you. With your default setting of a smile, kind facial expressions, welcoming behavior, and good manners, you are taking advantage of opportunities to display positive energy and peaceful intentions. You should stand at the church entrance both before and after Sunday Masses and at the door for other parish events in the hall or other common areas. The more you do this, the more you place your good intentions in the minds of people. This will produce a halo effect for you if there are ever questions about your behavior in the parish.

Make Time for Interruptions

As a parish leader, you have a lot of things going on and many responsibilities. Sometimes, understandably, it can be difficult to get them all accomplished on time. That can lead to your rushing from one event to another, walking swiftly along corridors or from one building to another. It's easy to get frustrated and say regrettable words when you are interrupted while working on an important project or rushing to your next meeting or other event.

Think for a moment how rushing or looking busy appears to other people. It might just convey the message "Don't even think about talking to me now!" Well, that is definitely not first saying peace! Perhaps it would be wise to consider how you schedule events so that you are not perennially rushed for time. Factoring in more time between events so that you will not feel the need to rush will be better for your frame of mind and convey a much better pastoral image to your people. It could be a very wise move to actually schedule time for interruptions and unexpected events so that you are less likely to brusquely brush aside a parishioner in need because you are late for the next thing.

Just Wave

A parish often has parishioners and visitors coming and going during the day. I have developed the practice of waving at every car that drives by when I am outside. Often, I cannot see the driver because of tinted windshields. But I know they can see me clearly, and likely don't know or think about the fact that I cannot see them, and thus may wonder if I was snubbing them if I don't wave. So I err on the side of being friendly. Waving a greeting at every car that passes might seem a small thing, but it is not. No one likes to be ignored, so wave at everything that moves!

Make Your Mission Statement Real

It is not enough to have a beautiful mission statement beautifully framed on the parish office wall. That mission must be lived out in concrete behavior by all those in your parish office who might see it every day, especially at the reception desk.

Greet Vendors and Workers

When your receptionist, office staff, and even schoolchildren greet vendors, groundskeepers, repairmen, custodians, and all visitors warmly, it sends a powerful message of welcome to people who are often ignored during their workdays. They might never receive this friendly greeting anywhere else. How wonderful for them to receive it at your parish! Help promote this practice by greeting these individuals with warm welcome whenever you see them and, if it seems appropriate, nudge others to do so as well.

Answer the Phone!

Office voice recordings that started as labor-saving measures have become simply annoying to most people. You may not realize it because you have ready access to whatever information you need since you are in the office. Those calling the parish office do not have this access and likely find recordings irritating and off-putting. Of course, it is best to have a real live person answer every call. Why not establish that expectation in your office and provide professional training for all those who answer calls? That initial human greeting can mean a lot to a first-time caller. Staff can easily direct calls regarding common questions to recordings containing the information being sought. You can also alert your staff to be especially patient with and welcoming of the high volume of calls around Christmas and Easter, and maybe even have additional help available to answer the phone at those times.

Your parish phone line is the face of your parish to many people, especially newcomers. Never underestimate the impact of an actual human answering it.

SAYING PEACE
THROUGH PHYSICAL PLANT
AND MESSAGING

It is not just people who communicate. Your parish's buildings, décor, signage, and messaging are important modes of communicating peace and welcome to parishioners and visitors alike.

Parish Buildings

Is there anything about your buildings that reinforces suspicions people have about the Church or causes people to feel nervous? It is good to take the time to objectively analyze your parish structures with those questions in mind. What you know well about your parish and its many activities, many people simply do not. Of course you know where the office, the church, and the restrooms are. You cannot assume that everyone coming to your parish does. Is your space clean and clear of clutter so that it says peace? Are necessary repairs made in a timely manner? Is the atmosphere comfortable, even pleasing, to be in? If people feel lost and their nervousness about being in a new place increases when arriving at your parish, this means that you have not communicated your peaceful welcome very well!

Your Office

Because you spend so much time there, you may have grown accustomed to your office and take it for granted that all is well with how it is arranged. Not so for all those who come to meet you! This may be their very first time ever in a parish office. They may bring with them past experiences of parish authorities that may be negative. Is it easy to find your office? Is your office cluttered, with papers and files all over the place? Are there comfortable places for people to sit? Is your office well lit? What might the pictures or decorative items you have displayed communicate to your visitors? Everything in your office will have an effect on everyone who comes in, so taking the time to reflect on what your office "says" is useful and helpful.

Signage

Imagine what it is like to come to your parish for the first time, not knowing anything at all about it. Will people know where to go for the school meeting, religious ed meeting, RCIA meeting, or even the funeral or wedding for their friend? Does your parish have easy-to-see directional signs? People do not like to feel lost, and highly visible signs that help them to go where they need to go signal peace and welcome in a beautiful way. Stop and think through, or better yet walk through and try to imagine, what a newcomer would notice or be looking for and not see. Then have someone with good design skills create the necessary signage to communicate peace and warm welcome.

Print and Digital Messaging

Take a close look at all your communication materials, and ask yourself if they are welcoming, useful, and easy to understand. Do they look as if care was used in creating them? How do your bulletins, pulpit announcements, website, and other social media present your parish? Imagine what impressions a visitor from another town might form about your parish. Are your people given enough advance notice about future events? Is it easy to sign up and participate? Are announcements written in clear English or complicated Church jargon? Parish ministries often have names that do not automatically reveal what they do. *Parish Outreach Ministry, Faith Formation, Evangelization Office,* and *Christian Service Ministry* are titles familiar to Catholic insiders but may not be to newcomers. What other language might communicate more directly to newcomers?

Catholic websites are very different from Protestant sites. Because of the vast variety among Protestant churches, their websites first feature the characteristics of the worship services (such as charismatic or fundamentalist), and *all are designed to welcome you in.* They say up front what you can expect at that church. Catholic Church services are more uniform, and so the home pages of Catholic websites often feature only Mass times and information about other sacramental preparation and celebration schedules, with various parish activities listed on the interior pages. This is true for Catholic bulletins as well. You might learn from other churches. Look around at other church websites and bulletins to glean ideas for your own parish website and/or bulletin. What do you like and not like about what others are doing to communicate parish life? Spend time researching the success of those around you, and imitate what you think works well.

Finally, you will want to make sure that your website and all your social media platforms feature your parish staff, along with their pictures and easy ways to contact them at the office. You might even include a welcome statement from each staff person and key volunteer leader across platforms. A video welcome from each would be fantastic! Make it very easy for people to connect with all your parish leaders.

SAYING PEACE TO THOSE WHO NEED IT MOST

Where is *first say peace* most important? Who might need to hear it most? Probably the parishioner who is wrong, mistaken, ignorant, foolish, forgetful, or even sinful. We have our Lord's own words affirming his role as the good doctor: "Those who are well do not need a physician, but the sick do. I did not come to call the righteous but sinners" (Mk 2:17). Of course, the most powerful words of all come from his Sermon on the Mount: "Love your enemies" (Mt 5:44). "The sick" are your very best opportunity for authentic evangelization. How you treat those in your parish who are weak, ignorant, wrongheaded, forgetful, and even sinful is a key way you can measure how you are doing as an authentic minister of the Gospel.

First of all, neither you nor any of your staff or volunteers should make statements such as these: "You should have read it in the bulletin! You should have heard the pulpit announcement! You should already know what our faith teaches!" Jesus, as always, is the example to follow.

The Look of Jesus

Our Lord met Matthew the tax collector and called him to be a disciple. Why did Matthew follow? The gospel indicates only that Jesus saw him (see Luke 5:27). Somehow Matthew felt acceptance and understanding in that look. Jesus would never condone the sinful behavior of tax collectors like Matthew, but he nevertheless communicated a message of peace. Perhaps that was the very first time a hated tax collector like Matthew had ever received such a gaze of love! It had a life-changing impact.

Parishes are filled with people who do not read the bulletin and do not know canon law, or the *Catechism*, or the requirements for godparents at a Baptism. They do not know marriage requirements or how to behave or dress in church. How do we look at them? Our Lord wants us to look at them as he looked at Matthew—with love.

Our desire to improve their behavior must begin with this look of love, which is the most beautiful mode of speaking peace. We must never pathologize people for their present faith condition! We take them where they are and help move them toward a fuller understanding of our faith, just as our Lord did with Matthew . . . and certainly does with us!

If Your Peace Is Not Received

Finally, our Lord provides profound practical advice for when our peaceful greeting is rebuffed, ignored, or rejected: "If a peaceful person lives there, your peace will rest on him; but if not, it will return to you" (Lk 10:6). He simply asks us to move on. We are not to take these rejections personally, nor are they to change our basic stance of saying peace at all times. Remember, we never let another's lack of love affect our love. Jesus profoundly respects human freedom; if people do not respond to our peace, we respect that and do not take it personally.

The next chapter will present how our Lord invites you to meet your people in a deeper way.

KEY TAKEAWAYS

- Jesus knows you are among wolves. He will always be with you!
- He also experienced what you experience now, carrying peace to a hostile world.
- Smile at everyone you meet to signal that you come in peace and mean no harm.

- Your peace and your love for your people will come from your relationship with our Lord.

2.
EAT WHAT IS SET BEFORE YOU

"Whatever town you enter and they welcome
you, eat what is set before you."

—Luke 10:8

KEY IDEAS

What might at first look like a reminder to be a polite dinner
guest is actually our Lord's call to you to learn the culture of your
community. The "foods" that nourish your people are all the
moral ideals, beliefs, priorities, values, and habits of behavior
that make up their culture—the attributes or characteristics that
make them tick.

Understanding a local culture takes time and much patient
observing, listening, and learning. But it is time well spent. Think
of the impact you will make as people recognize how you honor
them by taking the time to learn about and work to understand
them and how it is they live. Understanding culture is essential
before launching any program or strategic plan. A popular adage
in the business world and beyond is "Culture eats strategy for
breakfast." Specific parish cultures can be powerful enough to
swallow up even a brilliant strategic plan in one big bite.

Knowing the culture improves the chance that your interventions will be well placed, compelling, and effective. Knowing the culture is not the same as condoning it. After all, Jesus

meant to change the pagan culture of his time, and we are called to change ours—to help our world grow closer to Christ and embrace the saving power of his love.

Our Lord's words were direct and commanding: "Eat what is set before you." Hearing this instruction, the disciples probably worried about breaking Jewish dietary laws while in pagan towns. What if they were only served food that they were normally not allowed to consume? What might happen if they broke kosher? There were vast cultural differences between Jewish life and that of people in the Greco-Roman areas they were entering. Our seventy-two disciples would have seen theatres where locals would enjoy plays of a highly sexualized and immoral nature . . . and laugh about them. They would encounter a culture built largely around slave labor. They would see a culture centered on military might and intimidation of the weak. Fortunately, our seventy-two disciples knew that our Lord's deeper meaning was not to accept these ideas, but to engage, learn from, and come to understand the cultural differences that "nourished" the people they would meet. He wanted his followers to get to know the values, beliefs, and commitments of the people from whom they were so different.

Our Lord wants you also to understand your own people. He wants you to take time and make a good effort to get to know them and what's important to them. Nothing you do will last unless you develop a profound understanding of both the parish culture in which you are called to lead and the wider culture in which the parish exists. After all, you cannot evangelize people you do not know. So your next task after saying peace is to discover and understand your parish culture and what is important to your people.

Your parish is made up of people who, like all of us, want to be respected, valued, and appreciated. If you communicate respect and interest right away, you will bond quickly with your people. People remember how you make them feel, and nothing feels as good as being treated with dignity and respect, particularly by a leader about whom you may well have some skepticism. If you show parishioners respect from the very beginning of your time in leadership, no matter who they are or what their culture is, you will have a better chance of making a difference later on when you try to move them to a new place. Jesus had many dinners with Pharisees with whom he strongly disagreed, yet they felt comfortable to invite him to their homes! He must have made them feel respected simply as human beings, despite their obvious sinfulness.

Charging in with your own strategy right away will only communicate that you have not taken the time to learn where your people are *now* and how things are done *here*. It can communicate that you consider them too ignorant to see what you, in your wisdom, see right away. That often comes across as insulting. While it is true that you have power and authority as a parish leader to set a vision and plan for the future, even if only in a narrow bit of parish life and ministry, your people have all the local cultural information that you need to know in order to succeed. Take the time to get to know them and learn it from them!

WHAT IS CULTURE?

Culture is the totality of values, beliefs, and especially habits of behavior in any group of people. Quite simply, culture is "how things are done here." This includes all sorts of useful information, such as who makes decisions, how they are made, what the local traditions and customs are, and what is considered normal and abnormal behavior. You will need to know all this information to succeed in parish ministry. Finding answers to the following questions will help you get started. Consider taking notes or keeping a log of responses to the following.

- Who are the leaders in your parish?

  - Who are the people that your people listen to? Who can make things happen? Identify both the titled staff people (paid and volunteer) and also people who have significant influence but not necessarily an official leadership position.
  - How do people get into leadership or become influential?
  - How are complaints and disagreements handled, or not?
  - Are the leaders good listeners and responsive, or not?

- How are decisions made and communicated?

  - Is it clear who is in charge of each parish ministry?
  - Who participates in decision-making?
  - How are decisions communicated? Announcements after Mass? Emails? Parish bulletin or website? Shouting? Nothing?

- What are the different roles that people have in your parish?

  - Do you have civic leaders in your parish? How are they involved, or not?
  - Who are the biggest influencers? Why do they have that influence?
  - What are the cliques or factions of the parish that influence decisions?
  - Who are the people that seem *not* to have a voice? Why is this?

- What is the ethnic and racial makeup of your parish?

  - How do these groups interact, or not?
  - Which ones are dominant, and which are not?
  - Are the balances shifting?

- What are the economic levels in your parish?

  - How do these different groups interact, or not?
  - Which ones are dominant, and which are not?
  - Are these levels shifting in new ways from the past?

- What is considered normal and abnormal behavior in your parish and community?

  ◆ Is it a casual resort community? Working-class suburban? Professional-class urban? Informal rural? Casual, wealthy suburban?

  ◆ What is considered decent dress at Mass?

  ◆ What is the moral sense of your community? Liberal? Conservative? Hybrid? Mixed?

- What is unique about your parish?

  ◆ Are you near a tourist or historical attraction or an urban, rural or resort area, or perhaps a large military base that helps define the parish identity?

  ◆ What local economic, social, or political issues define your parish culture?

  ◆ What circumstances particular to your parish or your neighborhood help or hinder your mission?

- Most important: What is the marriage and family culture like in your parish?

  ◆ Do traditional marriage and family values predominate?

  ◆ Is there a significant nontraditional marriage and family community?

  ◆ Are marriages increasing, staying level, or decreasing? Why?

Culture Reveals the Narratives People Tell about Themselves

Narratives come from answering basic questions that seem to have been placed within each human person by God: "Why did this event happen in my life? Why is my life the way it is?" These questions are not only the origin of all science, but also the basis of personality development. We form stories or narratives that explain why we are as we are—for example, my parents affected me this or that way, my health issues changed me in this direction or that, and so on. People can see themselves as victors or victims depending on the story they have learned or developed about themselves, their families, and their wider community.

Parishes also develop narratives about how they are now and why. While a parish includes many individuals, it can also develop a unified story about itself. Perhaps it feels forgotten by the bishop, angry toward him, or especially blessed by him. Some parishes have particular challenges because of a downturn in the local economy, others are blessed by a new economic opportunity like the opening of a new factory or business. Many parishes, especially in the Northeast and Midwest, struggle with declining numbers and aging members, while others seem to be bursting at the seams with young families. Knowing the collective narrative of a parish is important for any ministry.

So culture reveals how people see themselves. We will explore much more about culture later in this chapter. For now, access your powers of imagination and ask yourself: "What must it be like to be a person living in this parish? How have all the issues raised in the list above molded the way they live? How would I feel if I lived in this culture?" The more you can see the world through the eyes of your people, the closer you will come to an accurate view of them, which is the basic starting point for any intervention or changes you might like to initiate later on.

Culture Is Powerful, Pervasive, Persistent, . . . and Massively Resistant to Change

You may have wonderful ideas and well-planned strategies in mind, but they will be useless and ineffective unless you take into account the local culture. The best-laid plans, clever slogans, and beautiful mission statements are never enough. Peter Drucker, one of the most respected observers of organizations in our time, famously liked to say "Culture eats strategy for breakfast!" The local parish culture will swallow up your plan quickly unless you take the time to learn the culture *before* creating that plan. After all, a parish culture has been around for a long time and is deeply ingrained. People may give lip service to a clever slogan but then revert right back to "how things are done here." You will need to take the time to learn about the people you seek to lead in order to be successful.

Let Love Motivate Your Cultural Curiosity

You can only evangelize people you love. Every love relationship begins with finding things out about people, and love must be your only motive for doing so. People go through this discovery process when they are dating and interested in forming a lasting relationship of love, which is also your goal as a parish minister. No one tries to change the other on the first date! You simply try to get to know the person better.

When you take the time to inquire about the joys, hopes, fears, and needs of your people, you show the interest and care that signal love. The first paragraph of *Gaudium et Spes*, the Second Vatican Council's *Pastoral Constitution on the Church in the Modern World*, is instructive here: "The joys and the hopes, the griefs and the anxieties of the people of this age, especially those who are poor or in any way afflicted, these are the joys and hopes, the griefs and anxieties of the followers of Christ."

Keep in mind this important and powerful concept. What is unique about our Lord's directive is that he asks you to get to know people whom you may not find very attractive! Jesus sent his disciples into pagan Greco-Roman territory and among some very hostile people—not a particularly inviting undertaking, I suspect. Today he calls you to leadership in a world with plenty of division and hostility, some of it within the very parish you have been called to serve. But these hostile and divided people are the very people who need the kingdom of God and God has chosen you to invite and lead them to discover it. Luke 10 Leadership provides you with the perfect plan for just that mission.

Jesus invites you to begin with a simple curiosity about the people you meet—to eat what is set before you, good or bad. In our own deeply divided culture, asking *why* people hold a different view engages them in wonderful ways and opens them up to the possibility of hearing the Word of God alive in their lives.

OBSERVE, LISTEN, AND LEARN

So how do you discover your parish's culture? By observing closely, listening carefully, and learning slowly. You try to see through the eyes of your parishioners and understand as if you were walking in their shoes.

Try to visit every place and event in the parish that you can—parish ministry meetings, school classrooms, club and association meetings, and the home of every parishioner who invites you to visit. The primary place and the premier event, of course, are the parish church and its weekend Masses. Here is where people will see you and meet you, where you can begin to know them and they can begin to know you. This can be exhausting, especially at the outset and particularly if you are introverted, but it will prove well worth the effort to be present and engaged at this gathering of the community.

Be Humble as You Collect Information

You will receive an enormous amount of information about all sorts of needs and issues from all kinds of people. Some information may be helpful, and some may be delivered with malicious intent. It may be hard to keep it all in order. Fair enough. But this is just your intake period of assessment, which means that you must withhold judgment about what you observe and discover for the time being. This first step is mainly a patient process of quietly observing your parish culture.

Patient listening requires a certain level of humility, of not assuming we have all the answers right away. Once when I was assigned to a new parish, I was besieged before I even arrived by several disgruntled parents wanting the school principal fired. I listened patiently to them for several weeks. I also interviewed the entire school staff in depth and, based on their input, decided to retain the principal, who went on to greatly increase enrollment and school success. I am glad I did not jump to conclusions based on the first impressions I received.

Here is another story to illustrate the importance of patience in getting to know the culture in which you are called to lead. There was once a well-educated man who considered himself the smartest person in the world. He heard about a monk on a faraway mountaintop with that same reputation, so he traveled across the world to meet the monk. He said to the monk, "Tell me something smart!" The monk responded, "First, we will have tea." The monk then began to pour tea into the man's cup, filled it to the brim, and even kept pouring as it overflowed. The man said, "Stop pouring! My cup is already full!" The monk replied, "Yes, so it is. And when you came to see me, your head was already full of ideas, and you had no room for mine."

Observing, listening, and seeking to learn imply an openness of mind that does not jump to conclusions but patiently waits for the larger story to unfurl and takes the time to understand it well from the viewpoint of the people you meet. That attentiveness will pay off. People care less about how much you know—and more about how much you care. Jesus knew that well, and so should you.

Lead by Receiving What Is Set Before You

Observing, listening, learning: these seem so passive—the opposite of what people often mistake for leading (being in charge or simply giving orders). But your choosing to observe, listen, and learn—to receive what is set before you—is actually a decisive program of active leadership. Your people will notice that you hear them and want to understand them well. They may not get what they want (or think they want), but they will know they have been heard and respected. And that experience will lead to mutual trust between them and you.

Observing and listening bring you instant information, much as rain falling on dry ground has an obvious initial impact: it pools and makes puddles. But only when the rainwater seeps slowly into the ground and reaches roots or seeds does real growth begin. The growth that comes with learning requires the slow process of contemplating what you have observed with your eyes and heard with your ears, and then making something good grow with what you have learned.

Observing, listening, and learning may also reveal deeper, unseen reasons for behavior that you may not understand at first. You may discover that a staff person's mysterious behavior is connected to the stress of caring for a sick relative, or their own health concerns, or a fear of new things, or anxiety over losing a job, or a complete misunderstanding of you and your ideas! You will not know such things if you do not take the time observe, listen, and learn. So, imagine yourself in his or her shoes. How would you feel if your boss sat down with you to discuss your work and you heard these questions?

- Will you help me better understand this parish, your job, and your role?

- Many people have questions about this parish; what are yours?

- Is there anything going on in your life that is impacting your time here?

- Do you have a sick relative or problems with kids or your spouse that affect you now?

- What can I do to help you minister more effectively and achieve your goals?

These are simple and practical examples of conversation starters through which you can glean valuable information from your staff.

These kinds of inquiries into what they value and worry about can open for you great opportunities to build trust as you come to know and receive the person in front of you. They help you stand in the other's shoes and see the world through her or his eyes.

Engage in Holy Conversations

Love comes from meaningful talk. People fall in love on dates when they reflect on their lives thus far and share hopes for their futures. Couples considering marriage draw closer to engagement when they talk together about where they might live, dream together about future children, and explore career plans. As you engage with parishioners on important topics, you will be entering into this larger context of their lives. You will hear their long-range parish plans, disappointments about failed parish projects, and hopes for their future lives. God designed us to feel close to people with whom we engage in this kind of meaningful talk about the big picture of their lives. God is present in such conversations, making them holy: "For where two or three are gathered together in my name, there am I in the midst of them" (Mt 18:20).

Hear the Bad Things Patiently

Your first impulse might be to interrupt and comment on that bad thing you just heard or saw taking place. This is certainly a common response, but one that doesn't often help. Interrupting usually only increases the resistant emotions of others. No one likes to be interrupted! Waiting for the whole story to unfold, even if you kind of know where it is going and so do those around you, communicates patience and respect. Listening means actually listening, not just waiting for your turn to talk! If you unfortunately do hear bad things, you are in good company with our Lord, who knew he was living in a world full of conflict and among hostile people, as his frequent dining with Pharisees revealed. You will see his patient response in the next chapters.

From my training in marriage and family therapy, I know that spouses will often present horrible behaviors and accusations about one another or some outside enemy. Wise counselors know to simply hold all that information in abeyance, in a kind of storage, waiting for the fuller story to emerge. It is the same when trying to learn a parish culture. Be patient in awaiting the more complete story.

Honor Cultural Differences

Often the most obvious cultural features of a parish are its distinctive ethnic and racial demographics. Frequently, these are also areas of great sensitivity, requiring that you be attentive to the characteristics, traditions, and values of various groups as well as their distinctive spiritual and pastoral needs. You must also be sensitive to the interactions between different groups and how your own background comes into play. For example, consider how your own racial, ethnic, and economic history and your own assumptions or biases factor in to the situation. Are you a minority leader? Are you from a dominant racial or ethnic group? Never discount the meaning and impact of either situation. It will always be an importatnt factor in who you are and in your approach to parish leadership.

Much has been written about these issues, and this book is not the place to analyze them in detail. If you have various ethnic and racial groups with particular needs and concerns within your parish, and certainly if there is conflict or tensions between groups, take the time to study and understand them as best you can from the many fine resources available. Of course, the best resources you have are the various groups themselves. You will learn who they are and what they value by getting to know them and allowing them to know you. Build genuine relationships rooted in Christian charity, and you will learn to understand and value the diversity of cultures within your parish culture.

DISCERN PERSONAL NARRATIVES

Each person you meet also has his or her own personal culture, or way of doing things. Like group culture, personal culture is based on the story or narrative that best explains to people the life they live. They may have a *victim* narrative, where they feel always attacked by others; or a *superior* narrative, where they feel above others; or a *humble* narrative, where they are eager to learn from anyone.

In your conversations, whenever you hear anything that sounds revelatory or interesting, simply say something like "That sounds fascinating. Please tell me more about that." If you want to initiate a more in-depth conversation, you might ask questions like "What do you enjoy about your life? Your family? Your job? This parish? What are your biggest frustrations and stresses these days? What kinds of things do you want to see happen in the parish?" Always remember that for many people the foremost concern is their status in the world or their sense of worth, dignity, and respect in their community. Therefore, you might keep in the back of your mind the question "Who does this person want to impress?" You can understand a lot about people and their behavior once you know whom they want to look good in front of and where they want to experience a sense of belonging.

Your people are also not static; they do not remain the same from one year to the next. Always stay engaged with them as individuals—perhaps even repeating the same questions as time goes on. Someone once asked Mother Teresa how she could minster to so many thousands of people. She simply replied, "I don't. I minister to one person at a time." That is how you must think as well. Each person you meet has a culture or narrative that explains his or her life. Discerning some of those individual narratives well and quickly will help you a great deal in being an effective minister.

Know Your Own Narrative

You cannot lead others if you do not know yourself, so you must know yourself well! You can actually interview yourself just as you would interview your staff or parishioners. What makes you tick? What nourishes you? What is your story? Who or what has shaped your values, your worldview, your beliefs, and even your daily habits or routines?

Listening to how your people experience you can help—and even be quite humbling. How are you known? Do you tend to run late, or are you always on time? Are you loud or quiet? A slow or a fast worker? Be humble enough to receive critique well. Because we leaders are afraid of what embarrassing things others might discover about us that may cause us to change, this is a part of leadership that rarely happens. Yet it is what you do not know or discover about yourself that has the potential of harming you most of all.

Sigmund Freud famously developed a theory of psychological analysis based on intense and honest self-disclosure and self-discovery. However, he never allowed anyone to question his own twenty-cigar-a-day habit. Ironically, it was the cancer, which developed from his cigar smoking, that eventually killed him. It is what we don't know that can harm us.

God's love for you can give you the courage to face yourself honestly. You must never fear what you find out about yourself, because you cannot change what you do not know. I have developed a corollary to the experience of Freud that I call Fr. Dave's Law.

Fr. Dave's Law

Anything you find out about yourself is good news! If you stumble upon once-hidden aspects of your life, your narrative, the personal culture in which you function each day, you can begin a plan to change yourself for the better. Just as what you don't know will harm you, what you do know can truly help you.

MY EXPERIENCE OF
PARISH CULTURES

After my ordination in 1978, I was first sent to a large parish that had an elementary school with seven hundred students and a high school with eight hundred students. There were several large factories and assembly plants nearby, and many of the parishioners were hard-working union members. They valued education as a way forward for their children, and their strong patriotism was fueled by gratitude for their prosperity. One of the largest Masses of the year in this parish was on Memorial Day. The parishioners and thus the parish culture were respectful of authority and the leadership chain of command within the parish.

My next assignment was to a small parish in a kind of artist community, with many writers, artists, and actors. It was a very informal parish in which everyone went by their first name, including the priests. I was startled at first but was glad to be patient and learn this local culture because I discovered that the informality of calling clergy by their first names was not disrespect, but rather great affection. The parishioners were also very proud that their parish had fairly equal numbers of Anglo, Hispanic, and black parishioners, with balanced numbers coming from lower, middle, and upper economic groupings. Everyone got along quite well across the diversities and distinctions.

Another parish was literally across the street from a large horse-racing track. You could hear the announcer calling the races during Mass! The track employed many of our people, and nearly all parishioners enjoyed visiting it. Racing was a topic of conversation almost every day. Having a large attraction like a track, amusement park, or other tourist destination in your parish can set a cultural tone that is important to know and understand well.

Another parish I served was filled with people who were leaders in industry and business. Almost the entire parish was college-educated, many with advanced degrees, and many of those from Catholic colleges. They knew their faith well. Learning their culture, I discovered a profound, well-informed spirituality. Rather than assume that the wealthy are selfish, I learned of their great generosity to the church. And they humbly looked to their parish for effective and practical spiritual guidance in the challenging world of business leadership.

Yet another parish contained mainly people in show business, where feelings and emotions are highly valued traits. These parishioners wanted parish events that were authentic and real, but presented with great passion and emotion; they wanted to be emotionally moved by their parish experience. There was an expectation that every liturgy would have outstanding music, singing, lighting, choreography, and an amazing sermon.

I was eventually blessed to be the pastor of a parish in the town where I grew up, in a beautiful area just north of Los Angeles. Many people moved to this place to find the perfect life for their families, so their standards for the parish were very high. Since many highly educated professionals were moving in all the time, I learned to provide clear and compelling explanations of parish events, parish policies, and Church teachings.

Lastly, yet another parish I ministered in was almost entirely Hispanic but also entirely English-speaking. It was in one of the oldest suburbs of Los Angeles, where generations remained together in the same area. On Sunday, you would see grandparents, their children, their grandchildren, aunts, and uncles all sitting together at Mass, and you knew they would also spend the rest of the day together. This was a parish community devoted to family and time spent together.

All these parishes were very different and made up of people with distinct values and priorities for their personal lives and the life of the parish. Each group had particular ways of doing things that expressed who they were and what they considered most important. Each parish set before me a wonderful feast of the beautiful particularities of their shared life. I remain grateful that God, in his infinite wisdom, kept me patient and open to receiving what was set before me.

Common Situations in Catholic Parishes

Catholic parishes seem to have some common cultural markers. For example, parish schools often take up a lot of parish land, money, time, and other resources. This often leads to insufficient attention, real or perceived, to the religious formation programs that serve parish kids who don't attend the parish school. Hard feelings and seething tensions, if not open conflict, can arise. If you discover this tension in your parish, study the situation to see how you can help bring dignity to every ministry.

Another marker that you should come to understand is staff relationships. Pay attention to how your parishioners regard any religious sisters, deacons, and priests who are part of the parish's leadership team or staff. Are they admired or distrusted in general as though they are a single entity? Or are they evaluated and inter-acted with as individuals? What is the relationship between the clergy and lay staff? Do the clerics enjoy higher esteem or greater deference than the lay staff members?

Each of the answers you discover here can help guide your behaviors as a parish leader. How these clerical and lay people are listed in your parish bulletin or referenced in your comments can help change people's perceptions of their ministries and statuses. Do you want a very hierarchical structure or more collegial? Your leadership behavior will be determined that answer.

Some parishes are open to new ideas and to changes, while others seem mostly closed and set in their ways. Is yours open or resistant? Are the pastor and his staff on the same page as most of the parish is in this regard? A deeply engrained attitude of "it's how things are done here" can be like a body's immune system: it stops any foreign ideas from entering. Beware of the common objections "We don't do it that way!" and "We've never done that before!"

Why not open yourself to as many good ideas as you can, even ones never discussed before? You will spread your specific burden of leadership across many willing people offering to help with their ideas. Of course, you will have the last say, but you will have the benefit of an interesting, innovative, creative, and maybe even brilliantly insightful cache of ideas that may be just what you needed to hear!

You can also discern the impact of the pastor's personality, which will shape parish culture. Some parishes have larger-than-life leaders who color every aspect of parish life, while other pastors are more unobtrusive, leading from behind the scenes. In the first, leadership is focused entirely on one person, while in the second it is diffused across all the different parish ministries, each probably working independently of the others.

Is your parish marked by conflict and division? Are there factions, sides, and cliques? If so, see if you can figure out the root cause and who the key players are for each group. Then seek ways to help these individuals move toward healthier, more productive, loving engagement with one another.

THE DISCIPLES LEARNED TO NAVIGATE ROMAN CULTURE

Ancient Romans were confused by the disciples of Jesus. Hearing only gossip and rumors, they formed false impressions that seem almost humorous today. Here are brief descriptions of just a few of the Roman misunderstandings and their suspicions of Christians that our ancestors in the Faith had to know and understand well.

- *Eucharist is cannibalism.* They heard about people consuming someone's body and blood. That could only mean they were cannibals.

- *Baptism is infanticide.* They heard about immersion in water as a dying to self. That could only mean Christians drowned their children.

- *"Brothers" and "sisters" means incest or adultery.* Romans cared only about their own families. They heard about Christians calling non–family members these affectionate names. How could Christians care for non–family members? They must have had immoral relationships with them! Yet that universal love for all slowly had a positive effect.

- *Christian medical cures are magical.* Romans valued strength and power, hated weakness, and so generally abandoned sick people as disfavored by the gods. They heard about Christians caring for sick people who then got well. They must have had some special magical powers!

- *Open table fellowship is chaos.* Romans associated only with people of their own social rank. They heard that men, women, slaves, rich, and poor all gathered together at table and at worship. That was chaos! Yet that universal acceptance of all became attractive over time.

Despite all these terrible misconceptions, the patient and courageous ministry of the early Church was able to slowly and effectively counter all of these. Despite awful first impressions and fears, by the year 313, the Roman emperor Constantine personally and publicly accepted Christianity. By 380, Christianity had become the official religion of the empire. What caused this amazingly fast transformation, begun just a few centuries earlier with the compassionate and courageous behavior of Christian men and women from the time of Luke? We can summarize these Luke 10 Leadership steps so far. They all signaled love.

The leaders and populace of Rome had learned that the followers of Jesus were indeed sincerely interested in their well-being and in all their joys, hopes, and concerns. Christians seemed honestly interested in Roman culture and wanted to understand it well. Unlike Freud, they also allowed themselves to be completely transparent to their Roman neighbors. Romans therefore saw that these early Christians meant no harm, had come in peace, and sought sincerely to get to know the Roman culture. The Romans had experienced the first two steps of Luke 10 Leadership.

TODAY'S ANTI-CATHOLIC CULTURAL MISUNDERSTANDINGS

Today, we see five realities that have made many people suspicious of Catholics, including even some Catholics growing suspicion of the Church itself. They are happening right now and have brought tremendous harm to our faith and to religion in general. We need the guidance of Luke 10 Leadership now more than ever.

- *Church scandals.* This has been our greatest challenge by far. Both selfish religious leaders who perpetrated sexual crimes and, worse still, the supposed normal religious leaders who should have stopped them *but did not* have caused major harm to the reputation of the Church.

- *Terrorist acts done in the name of religion.* When terrorists justify violent murder and mayhem as ordered at the direction of God, major harm is done to the reputation of all religions.

- *The false belief that faith and science are opposed.* Fundamentalist readings of scripture seem to oppose what can be verified about the universe with research, observation, and common-sense. This religious repudiation of good science gives religion a reputation as a fairy tale. In Catholicism, there is never a "science and faith" opposition. After all, the God who made the universe cannot be in opposition to it.

- *The sense that the Church is opposed to same-sex couples, LGBT communities, and pro-choice groups.* People today, especially in Western countries, have an innate and admirable sense of fairness and equality regarding relationships between people who are in love. Denying full marriage to these groups comes across as unfair and unjust. People do not want to "impose" any values over another's values.

  Some think that the Church is opposed to people with same-sex orientation. While the Church encourages love between all people no matter who they are, its reservation of marital love to one man and one woman often comes across as denigrating the expression of any love and friendship for another person of the same sex.

The Church's stance on abortion and its affirmation of a right to life for the unborn can sometimes appear heartless toward pregnant women in dire circumstances of poverty or even rape. The Church's total affirmation of all life and especially the importance of the welfare of the mother under stress is often missed.

- *The rise of "nones" (those who identify with no religion).* Many of these people are agnostic about *any* institution. The millennial generation is strongly anti-institutional and suspicious of authority, whether in religion because of Church scandals and Islamic terror, politics because of corruption, or business because of the economic downturn of 2008 that arose from institutional greed.

  Since all these institutions had presented themselves as trustworthy sources of truth, many young people now distrust any authority that preaches objective truth. Perhaps chief among them is the Church.

Millennial and Generation Z Anti-Institutional Culture

Everyone today wants to understand millennials—those born roughly between 1981 and 1996—and Generation Z, which immediately follows the millennials. Many have already observed, listened to, and sought to understand these generational cohorts, which make up the largest segments of our population today. So what is it like to be a person in these generations? Generalizations are broad, but here are my reflections.

These are both generations who were highly chaperoned through childhood, and carefully supervised by parents in many aspects of their life growing up. They were driven to school, driven to after-school events, and supervised at all times. Parents even arranged their children's time with friends by scheduling playdates, also carefully monitored by adults. Their whole life was supervised and arranged.

This is why socialism seems so popular today among these two groups. Someone else, the government, a kind of "super parent" is completely taking care of many of them, paying their bills, ensuring their minimum wage, and offering many other free benefits.

This is vastly different from the experience of earlier generations of children, who were simply told to go outside and play after school and who would most of the time safely do so. Children in those earlier times were expected to learn to negotiate on their own how to make friends, create their own entertainment, handle bullies, deal with setbacks, celebrate victories, and find their own happiness. Certainly many did not navigate all of those interactions well, while others did.

You should remember that it was largely out of a deep love and sincere desire to protect their children from any harm that parents shielded them from these normal up-and-down challenges of life. But this deeply loving behavior had unintended side effects. Protective parental supervision can inadvertently signal to children that the world outside their home is dangerous and unsafe. These new generations therefore have a deep-seated experience of avoiding both being hurt by this outside world or ever hurting others

They experience objective and always-true moral guidelines as rules that hurt people because they restrict people's behavior. For example, they might have a gay friend who wants to marry a partner and thus consider the Church's objection to gay marriage as hurtful to their friend. Therefore, they conclude that Catholic moral ideals cannot be a good thing!

Their sense that overall objective moral rules are hurtful has led many in these generations to become moral relativists. They have a very difficult time accepting the concept of absolute truth. (Ironically, when they propose that there is no absolute truth, they are stating something they believe to be absolutely true!)

You should recognize with some degree of compassion for this generation that a self-identity of not wanting to be hurt or to hurt others can come across as extremely positive to young people. Who wants to be hurt or hurt others? This can appear to young people as profoundly noble. It is good to keep in mind that this worldview is very powerful and difficult to change.

I hope this understanding can also keep older generations from being unduly negative about the young. After all, they believe they are doing a noble thing by holding to their ideals.

STARS—KNOW YOUR PARISH TYPE

All of your observing, listening, and seeking to understand your people will give you a wealth of useful information. Gradually, you may begin to recognize some patterns, develop a general idea of the nature of your parish community, and see an overall picture of your parish. So now what? How are you supposed to respond?

Our Lord offers good advice in the parable of the sower, which is in all three gospels, so it must be important! (See Matthew 13:1–23, Mark 4:1–20, and Luke 8:4–15.) Scripture scholars tell us that all of our Lord's parables had some aspect that did not exactly ring true to listeners in his time, which made them more memorable. In this one, his audience knew that no farmer would scatter highly valuable seed haphazardly across all kinds of land. A farmer would carefully choose the right places to plant and see that the land was ready before scattering the seed, ensuring as best as possible a good harvest.

So it must be with you as well. Know your land—your parish culture and the subcultures within it—well so that you can prepare it for the seed that you will plant. Wise leaders know how to direct their efforts based on parish conditions.

Michael Watkins, writing in the January 2009 edition of *Harvard Business Review*, proposes that all communities fall into five types and that determining which type your community is can help you plan what to do next. I have adapted Watkins's framework here to help you assess your parish community and discern what will *nourish* it in the future. The five parish types form the acronym *STARS*:

S = **Sustained Success:** Your parish is already successful and can continue as is.

T = **Turnaround:** Your parish is in very deep trouble and needs rescue.

A = **Accelerated Growth:** Your parish is seeing big economic or sociological changes.

R = **Realignment:** Your parish just needs adjustments to an already good program.

S = **Start-Up:** Your parish is brand new and thus fertile ground for dynamic growth.

I explain the different types below, giving their stereotypical features and offering initial tips on getting to know and leading each one.

Sustained Success

This parish has been doing very well for some time. The people are well aware of their success, and you can be sure they are proud of their reputation . . . and so are naturally concerned about you! Certainly announce that you will keep everything as is and that all programs will continue. This is not the time to make major changes since the people do not feel anything is broken and you do not have the credibility yet to do so. You may not even know yet why it has been successful, so you might consider interviewing everyone on staff on the topic. You may find out that the reason for the parish's success is not what you might think at first, such as a dynamic pastor or great wealth. Finding out what has worked will be important. In the meantime, give lavish praise and credit to the parishioners and staff for what you see. Specifically mention what you like and whom you find impressive as well. People like to be complimented!

Turnaround

This parish is in deep trouble and needs a savior for immediate rescue. The people know that all is not well and look to you to make it all better, and fast. This is not a parish in which you should delay decision-making. However, you may not know exactly what went wrong and why things are so bad, so just make some quick, easy, and obvious changes that you sense everyone will support. Those quick "early wins" will give you credibility as a leader who cares and will lead your people to success. Those first needed corrections will also help buy you time to discover what went wrong and what the long-term solutions might be. Frequently, a parish goes downhill because of bad leadership, which is why so many people leave. Be careful of showing any arrogance or implying that you are so much better than the former leaders. *Never speak badly of your predecessors.* You must remember that the people who are still there when you arrive may be those who like it the old way. After all, they stayed! Your early wins that everyone likes will help your credibility and give you time to get them on board with your program.

If you are replacing someone removed for an allegation of sexual or other criminal misconduct, you have a parish in need of special sensitivity, particularly listening skills. Depending on what stage the case has reached (early investigation or after final court judgment), you must be careful to stay within the law and basic decency regarding what you say about the former leader and any victims. It might be good to remind your people about diocesan safeguards in place for the protection of children and your parish human resources standards. Your main task is to refocus the parish on hope for the future.

Accelerated Growth

This parish is undergoing rapid changes in one or more areas of your parishioners' lives. There could be massive layoffs at a major local factory or a brand-new factory offering sudden prosperity. There could be a major increase in immigrants arriving in town, a major decrease in population, or perhaps a demographic change abruptly leading to new political priorities and values. You will want to develop the skill to present any new challenge as an opportunity.

New unemployment could offer the opportunity to establish a new social networking program, help for the poor, and job fairs at your parish. Make sure these opportunities are real and not just wishful thinking. New employment means new parishioners, so direct your staff to develop new and innovative ways to connect with them. New politics can mean a new focus on the Church's moral positions and on ways to effectively communicate them, such as town halls, articles, speakers, and Catholic adult education classes.

Sudden changes are always new opportunities! However, people often do not like sudden changes, so a calm, assured, and confident manner is your very powerful signal to your people that all will be well.

Realignment

This parish is doing well but may need some minor adjustments here or there. This parish is a less intense version of a turnaround parish. Frequently, a realignment parish has been on cruise control for some time and is simply doing the same things year after year. It is kind of a zombie parish going forward without much direction or purpose. No one is complaining because there are no glaring problems, but no greater goal or purpose has been presented. This is a parish that needs to be realigned with the mission of our Lord to fulfill the kingdom of God.

You do not want to disparage the parishioners or indicate that anything in the parish is wrong, but rather gently invite them to a new level of activity that reveals how our faith helps them in practical ways. This is the easiest parish type in that there is no big problem to solve and no deep emotional issue in the parish. You only have to present the goodness of the kingdom of God!

Start-Up

This parish is brand new and offers you a great chance to begin well. It needs leaders who, like good farmers or gardeners, know how to prepare the land and sow the right seed for a great harvest. Not everyone can do this, so diocesan officials should take care to send the right person to start a new parish.

You will have the chance to establish the parish culture ("how things are done here") just the way you want. While that is an incredible opportunity to do good, it also can focus too much energy on you. Beware of developing a cult of personality where you start taking on a celebrity role, particularly if you are a pastor. You might consider establishing strong volunteer leadership across ministries to support your professional staff and helping build a strong, clear role for the pastoral council. Both groups can be crucial advisors, key supporters, and important sources of information. A good place for a pastoral council to start is to establish policies and procedures that will outlast your time there. That will demand a certain amount of humility on your part as well.

WHAT'S NEXT?

You have spent a lot of time observing, listening to, and learning from your people. You have a sense of what kind of parish you lead. Certainly there are some things you like and want to continue, but other things bother you. You may need to make some changes! Leading for change begins in our next chapter.

KEY TAKEAWAYS

- Eating what is set before you means discovering your people's culture and what nourishes them.
- Culture is the totality of values, beliefs, and especially habits of behavior in any group of people, or simply "how things are done here."
- You discover culture by observing, listening to, and learning what nourishes your people.
- Your cultural curiosity signals your interest in, respect for, and love for your people.
- Know the culture before starting any strategy: "Culture eats strategy for lunch!"
- Discover your parish's specific STARS type.

3.
CURE THE SICK

"Whatever town you enter and they welcome
you, . . . cure the sick in it."

—Luke 10:8–9a

KEY IDEAS

This is where you do something helpful right away. Curing the
sick does not only mean a miraculous event. Doctors cure people all the time using normal means of medical care. You can
do the same about an immediate and obvious parish problem
using good, old-fashioned practical solutions. This can be the
first time you take action to make something good happen for
your people. They will notice what you decide, how you go about
communicating your decisions, and how you make them happen. You will want to provide some immediate winning solutions
to real problems that you can be sure everyone will support.

You have already arrived in peace and taken the time to get
to know your people personally as well to learn to understand
your parish's overall culture and type. You know what makes
them tick, and you know better what makes you tick. Your observing, listening, and learning well has hopefully revealed the problems that your people are most concerned about right now.
Focus on those immediate and obvious concerns as soon as you
are able to do so without rocking the boat too much. Yes, you can

help bring healing to those who need it and also offer cures to situations that have become annoyances within your community!

You might think it unfair that our Lord's disciples had the advantage of performing miraculous cures to help their ministry flourish. Miracles certainly get people's attention! People lined up in front of the house in Capernaum where Jesus was staying after word got out that he cured Peter's mother-in-law (see Matthew 8:14–15, Mark 1:29–31, and Luke 4:38–41). Of course people would come running! Later that same day, Jesus stated that his mission was actually *not* to perform miracles but rather to announce the kingdom of God. This tells us that something else is going on in Jesus' command to cure the sick. He does not mean only miraculous physical healings. After all, doctors cure and heal people every day using standard medical procedures. Our Lord's statement means that you can bring healing on many levels and perhaps even cure a problem for good with ordinary but still very effective ministry habits and gospel-centered behaviors.

TARGET A PARISH PROBLEM THAT NEEDS ATTENTION RIGHT AWAY

Emergency room doctors first look at all that needs to be done and then prioritize treatment. This process is called *triage*, from an old French word for "sorting." Doctors want to make sure they handle the most urgent, serious cases first and do not take time away from emergencies to treat less important problems. In a similar manner, you can and should practice triage for your parish or ministry. In your situation of "cure the sick," triage means fixing the obvious and easy problems first and perhaps beginning a process for fixing the harder ones at a later time. Jesus often cured a person of physical illness but recognized that healing one person's damaged body is easier than healing a damaged and sinful culture. Both are important, of course. In your case, quickly curing your people's most immediate and obvious parish or ministry problems will demonstrate that you have come in peace with real and practical solutions. This is very important and profoundly effective as you arrive!

You have just been put in charge of some aspect of parish life or, if you are a pastor, oversight of all of parish life, and your people will want to see something tangible showing that the parish or ministry has new and promising leadership. They also might know best where the problems are, so consult with your people: listen to them, and ask for their suggestions and insights about what needs are most urgent. Doing something right away that solves a problem or cures an ailment in the life of the parish communicates that you want to do good things for your people and care for their needs. It shows that you have observed, listened, and learned well through your cultural curiosity and exploration and conveys your good judgment. By setting an environment and culture of care and revealing that you are a problem solver, you build trust and credibility.

If You Do Nothing

Despite the popular advice about not making changes for a full year when taking a leadership position, if you don't make some positive contribution to the parish within your first weeks as leader, you risk being seen as uncaring and unaware of both obvious problems with uncomplicated fixes and the needs of your people. Parishioners will see you as someone who has not observed, listened, and learned well. You may lose any goodwill that people are willing to give you as a new leader. People look to you to make their lives better in some way. If you ignore problem situations or do not take any action at all, you will soon be dismissed as ineffective, and that reputation is very hard to shake.

Shaping Your First Decisions

So your first steps are crucial, and securing early wins is an effective way to establish your potential to become a very successful parish leader. This is the moment where you first step up to actually do something for your parish. Everyone knows you have the power as a leader and will be noticing how you exercise that power.

Let's be clear up front. Decision-making is an exercise of your power and authority. There is no getting around that. But remember that your power and authority are the same kind that our Lord entrusted to his first disciples. Never be reluctant about using this power or too eager for it. We will discuss your feelings about power and authority later in this chapter, but they are central to your role as a leader right now. What is our Catholic understanding of power? It is the ability to make something good happen as God has designed. You have been given authority and power for the purpose of doing something good. I hope you will never see it as a burden but rather as an opportunity to create happiness through spiritual growth in the lives of your people. You have already taken a lot of time getting to know your people by observing, listening, and learning. That effort can build both compassion for their needs and courage to make those sometimes-difficult decisions on their behalf.

People will certainly see how you use the power and decision-making authority that comes with your leadership position. Do you rush to judgment, or carefully and thoughtfully plan a well-considered decision? Do you make decisions that clearly rise from your compassion for their needs? What "filters" do you use on the information that people bring you or that you discover through research? Who do you listen to and why? What sources do you trust?

You also need to consider when you make a decision, how collaborative it is, how you communicate it, and what its impact will be. Wise leaders take into account the ways in which each decision might be misunderstood. Never underestimate the power of people to completely misunderstand your message! Try it out first on trusted coworkers for their reactions and review.

Remember that people will be able to tell if you exercise authority for some self-aggrandizing or selfish purpose, so make sure your motives are clear and in line with what your people need, what the Church calls us to do, and who Eucharist reminds us to be each week.

Be careful about spending money on yourself or your office right away. This will only come across as selfish, especially if parish needs are mounting. Putting your needs off for a later time is money well *not* spent!

Leadership Styles

Consider whether you will make decisions in a top-down manner or collaboratively. Do you see yourself as leader sitting at the top of a pyramid of power or at the center of a web or wheel? You can encourage ideas from everyone involved in the area touched by whatever decision you are working toward making, or you can choose to be the only source of ideas and decisions. Different decisions will require different styles of exercising authority and leadership. Always remember to choose wisely and deliberately which path to take in reaching a decision—the path that will most effectively resolve the problem at hand.

One example of a collaborative leadership style from the corporate world is Pixar Animation Studios. Pixar enjoys an astounding record of success, having created the *Toy Story* series along with many other highly successful films. The company has developed an effective culture of creativity and innovation in which they bring many minds together to look at a new story idea with freedom to offer whatever contributions they want to. Pixar's leaders famously believe that a creative idea can come from anyone, anytime, and anywhere. Therefore, they value anyone who has an idea anywhere at any time. Everyone in the company, from the janitor to the secretary to the CEO, feels valued. They know they can contribute, and they know they will be listened to. Ideas may have to go through a lengthy vetting process, but all ideas are welcome for consideration, and the person offering the idea is treated with respect and gratitude.

Make Sure You Cure the Right Problem!

I hope you are motivated to make some early decisions. However, take care in choosing what to do. It's not always easy to discern what it is most prudent to tackle! In your observing, listening, and learning, you may discover that people give lip service to changes they would like but are not actually ready for those changes. People sometimes get used to a situation and would rather complain about it than make the needed changes. Choosing the right problem to cure is important. Jesus knew that well, as we see in the following story recounted in John 5:1–18.

Jesus arrives at the pool of Bethesda in Jerusalem, which archeologists tell us is actually two large reservoirs of water that officials occasionally transferred from one pool to another. Many sick and infirm people are gathered there because there is a tradition that whoever enters the water first after the transfer of water takes place will be healed. Jesus encounters a man who tells Jesus that he has been ill for thirty-eight years and that he has never been able to make it into the water first. Jesus asks him, "Do you want to be well?" That sounds like a strange question, but perhaps Jesus wonders if the man really wants healing at all. Would he perhaps rather just remain in the condition he is in? Maybe change is too hard. This remains a great question to ask in your parish. Always seek to understand the actual depth of desire and the real motivation for change. Once that seems clear, ask yourself whether the change will make the situation better and bring your people closer to Christ.

Recognize that you can only manage small changes at the beginning. It is too early to understand the bigger issues and know how to lead your parish in regards to them. It is also too early for you to have enough credibility for any large move. This is the time for a minor change that you can do right now and that your people will see as helpful but not very disruptive.

If any big change is obviously needed, then that is, of course, your first focus. But to be successful, big changes will demand a comprehensive and carefully thought-out process. You will probably be able only to start a process of change for those big problems now. My earlier book, *Motivating Your Parish to Change*, offers a step-by-step process for leading large and successful parish changes that will take your parish or ministry to a new place. It is based on the leadership example of Moses, who led his people through amazing and extraordinary challenges to leave behind their old ways in Egypt and successfully arrive in the new Promised Land.

When I arrived as pastor at one parish, I found that a recent church remodel had inadvertently placed a very ugly architectural feature between the tabernacle and the altar. In my entire priesthood, I have never before or since encountered a parish in which there was virtually 100 percent dislike for a structure! I learned the story of how it came to be there and understood the inadvertent causes of what was now an obvious problem. In my Sunday homilies during my second weekend in the parish, I told a bit of that story and promised the people that the problematic structure would come down and be replaced. This caused an instant standing ovation at every Mass! I was even somewhat grateful for this obvious problem that pointed to an easy first "cure" in my new role.

THE PROBLEM, THE SOLUTION, AND HOW YOU SAY IT

Big or small, the process for implementing change is always the same. You must clearly reveal the problem, showing how bad it is and why it needs fixing, even if it is an obvious issue. You must clearly explain your solution, showing how it will make things better. Most importantly, you can best do both by using the most effective form of communication ever: a great story that involves people facing and solving problems. True stories are always the best. Can you frame your decision in terms of a story of actual people finding success? Jesus is your model once again.

In telling the story of the Good Samaritan in Luke 10:25–37, Jesus is responding to a terrible lack of concern among religious leaders for those in desperate need. A Pharisee confronts Jesus with a direct question, possibly even sarcastically made: "And who is my neighbor?" Recognizing the antagonism, Jesus chooses to engage the Pharisee's imagination by telling a story rather than giving a lecture, which would probably have been ignored anyway. Jesus knows that even his enemies love stories. Jesus also gets the Pharisee to come up with the conclusion himself—always an effective teaching technique, and one I employ often.

When I arrived at one parish as a new pastor, I learned that there was tremendous concern about safety at the school, especially in light of so many horrific school shootings. I gathered different groups of parents together, narrated the story of their children walking into our schoolyard, and asked, "What would keep your children safe?" Their answer was a fence, and so it was a simple early win to install a new fence around the school, along with security cameras. Students would now be far safer than they had been before.

Open Up Your Communication Style

People are well aware that you have a lot of authority and can change parish life in dramatic ways. Many Catholic parishioners feel vulnerable because of the immense authority that pastors and other ministry leaders have. How well will you keep them informed? The better you communicate, the better off everyone will be. Bring your parishioners along in your decision-making process.

Help them know they are included. Let them know what you are thinking about and what affects your decision-making process. Are you open and transparent about what you are working on? Do you let your people know how and why you make the decisions you make? How do you let them know? Pulpit announcement, bulletin notice, parish-wide letter, social media, or the parish website? Are you open to questions and comments? If not, why not?

Like it or not, you are in the communication business. You can never *not* communicate, nor can you communicate enough! In the ancient world, the gods were mysterious and far away. Think of how Jesus' words from John 15:15 would have sounded in his disciples' ears: "I no longer call you slaves, because a slave does not know what his master is doing. I have called you friends, because I have told you everything I have heard from my Father." So it must be with you as a parish leader. Robust communication greatly increases your chance of success with the changes you want to make.

In one parish where I served as pastor some years ago, we had a big problem with gossiping parents. The gossip included vicious criticism of teachers and school policies. The situation was toxic and threatened the well-being of the school community. In consultation with the principal, I introduced a three-question survey in the weekly parent envelope: "What do you like about our school this week? What do you not like about our school this week? What are your solutions?" All of the comments would be typed up unedited, but without names attached, and sent back out to all parents in the next school envelope accompanied by the principal's very professional response to each complaint. The complaints were thus made public, so that every school parent could soon see the complaints compared to the very professional responses from our principal. The gossipers soon came to be seen as outliers and soon lost influence.

One area of parish management that is often opaque to parishioners is financial management. Many do not understand what happens to their donations after they place them in the basket at Mass on Sunday, and they want to know. Many do not know how the weekly collection is related to the funding of the local diocese. It's safe to assume that many have concerns about whether their financial support of the parish is somehow funding the legal costs and settlements arising from lawsuits regarding sexual and financial abuse in the Church. One of the very first things I have done within the first two months of beginning as pastor at each parish I have served was to write up an accurate description of parish and diocesan finances. This was placed in every bulletin and at the doors of the church. It was also included in our annual financial report to the parish every year afterwards. Once people understood that parish donations, by law, can be used only for parish expenses, they felt better that their donations were going where they wanted them to go.

Communication Means Actually Being Heard!

Just because you have said something does not mean it was heard well, or even heard at all! Leaders too often fail to notice or discern whether their message ever made it accurately to their listeners. This is the most common mistake in parish communication. It does not matter only what you say, but only what is heard.

Leaders obviously know both what they want to say and the entire context of their message. Unfortunately, leaders often shortcut their messages, thinking that people will automatically know what they mean. Well, they often don't! They cannot read your mind and so cannot know up front the whole context of your message. After saying something important, ask, "Can you tell me what you heard?" You may have to help your audience follow what you mean.

Moreover, differences in culture, ethnicity, generational cohort, gender, and even philosophical or political outlook can be barriers to effective communication. Oftentimes, men listen to women differently than women listen to men. Different cultures and ethnic groups have different communication styles, as can liberals and conservatives, and certainly there are distinctions between generations when it comes to communication styles. If you have ever wondered why what you thought was an amazing message was not received well across the board, it might be that you did not take into account one or more of these differences. It may also simply be that you have lived most of your life in a different part of the country and the local culture is still new to you. There is much written on these ideas, so take some time to review that literature. This will certainly be time well spent!

Whenever you speak, think about your listeners before you think about your message. What is already on their minds? When your people arrive at Mass on Sunday or at any meeting that you call, they are already immensely preoccupied with many things in their own lives and not necessarily thinking about the gospel reading or your message at the meeting. They might just have had an argument with their spouse, their kids, or their boss. They might be worried about their job, their weight, or their health. They may wonder why they are even coming to Mass or your meeting! If you do not recognize all these ideas already in their heads and your ideas do not align with what is already weighing on them, your ideas will simply bounce off as irrelevant.

JESUS COMMUNICATED AND CURED WITH PARABLES

Jesus, our example in all things, was a carpenter . . . *but he told no carpentry parables!* He rarely, if ever, spoke from his own experience but rather into the experiences of the people he addressed in his ministry. He told stories that related to the lives of farmers and fishermen; he told stories they would understand. When you prepare your remarks for whatever kind of communicating you need to do, think about what happened in the news this very week or what you might have learned about your parishioners in the last day or two. To be able to do that, you must daily know what is going on in the wider world and in the world of your people. If there is a huge news event that you sense will be uppermost on your people's minds, then think about how you can use it to make your point while also communicating that you know what concerns them most.

Remember the foundational event of the Incarnation when God became a human person, descended into our world, and entered into our human life speaking the language of fishermen and farmers (see Philippians 2:5–11). You must learn to become as the people you address and enter their lives as your own. Use the everyday and normal language they know; consider carefully before using the often esoteric jargon of official Church language. We treasure Church tradition, of course, but also recognize that it is often hidden in difficult-to-understand theological jargon or translated awkwardly from the official Latin. Language can divide or unite. Make sure you use it clearly and understandably to unite your people around the authentic message of our Lord, especially as you apply it to some immediate parish need.

Parables of Mercy

The immediate need Jesus recognized was that people felt a burden of condemnation for their sins; he sensed that they felt there was no possibility of salvation, as God would not want them. He cured the spiritually sick of his time through his famous parables of mercy, found in Luke 15, which we'll review briefly here.

In three dramatic and even shocking images, Jesus reveals who he is and how he views his mission. Each parable presents a person going to extraordinary lengths to connect with people in need. Besides using local scenes and events, the parables had another feature that captured attention: each parable had something wrong with it. The people at that time would have recognized that something was just a bit off, which made it stand out even more.

Parable of the Lost Sheep (see Luke 15:1-7)

This seems at first a heartwarming tale of an adorable sheep and a caring shepherd. However, Jesus' audience knew that *sheep rarely get lost!* They are the most timid of animals. If a sheep ever did get lost on its own, well, it must be an abnormal sheep. You would not want it back! Moreover, people who saw a shepherd returning with a sheep would have assumed he had stolen it, a crime then punishable by death. Jesus, the Good Shepherd, is willing to risk death to bring back a sheep that no one else wants!

Parable of the Lost Coin (see Luke 15:8-10)

People in Jesus' time placed straw in their houses at night to help cushion their sleep; they also brought their livestock, such as sheep and donkeys, inside at night for safekeeping. Each morning they would sweep out the old straw, dirty from animal droppings. The parable says the woman's search for the coin is at night, during the time when animals were inside. She is searching through dirty straw! By this parable, Jesus is telling just the sort of sacrifice he is willing to make in his search for us when we are lost.

Parable of the Lost (Prodigal) Son (see Luke 15:11-32)

This most famous parable is packed dense with insights; I will feature one that reflects our first Luke 10 Leadership step of *first say peace.* When the father sees his lost son returning he runs out to greet him warmly! In the ancient world, where fathers received great respect from their sons and not the other way around (in fact, a disrespectful son could face death), this would have been a profound reversal of roles. Yet the father understood his son's admission of sin as an amazing reversal of life and knew his son was deserving of mercy and forgiveness.

COMMON PARISH ILLNESSES

As a parish leader, you want to get good things done for your people. Here are some common parish problems that get in the way, along with some very short interventions that hopefully can help you make some quick cures.

Bad Meetings: Time Is Being Wasted

Calling people together for a meeting is actually the very definition of Church. The Greek word for *Church*, *Ekklesia*, meaning "called out," referred to a gathering or assembly of people called out from their homes for some common purpose. The necessity of coming together for Mass is clear enough since we know our Lord calls us together for that. Mass is a time for listening to the Word of God in the scriptures, prayers, hymns and homily. It is also a time for responding to our Lord and receiving him in the Blessed Sacrament so that we are made new. The purpose of parish meetings is often less clear. Meetings can fall into a deadly routine in which they happen only because it is the regular date for them. They often accomplish nothing.

If you manage or direct a group of volunteer ministers, it is best to make sure you and the group know why you are all there and not doing something else. Your team members need to know what is expected of them at every meeting and what tasks need to be accomplished—and those pieces of information come from you, their leader. Such meetings can work well when you invite people together for a clear and necessary purpose, with a clear role and clearly communicated expectations for each person involved. Do you want input on a special topic that only these people can provide? Do you want to communicate special information to just these people? Do you want to assign specific tasks? If you communicate those ideas ahead of time, then you will have great meetings!

Bad Finances: Money Getting in the Way

Money is simply the power to do something good. However, too much focus on money can turn your people off, and too little can make them nervous that bills are not being paid. If you ever need to ask for donations, remember that your people are not simply a means to your ends, as good as those ends might be. As donors, they should feel they are coworkers with you in making a well-considered and needed project happen. You want to make sure that you are asking people to donate to a worthwhile and legitimate parish cause *that enables them to help* advance the kingdom of God. You are asking them for donations precisely and *only* to help them fulfill God's plan for salvation. This is a judgment call you make about the cause you are promoting and your motives for doing so, whether as pastor or leader in charge of your ministry's budget. You will also want to be able to make that case with reasonable explanations and justifications.

Make sure you present an accurate financial report every year, and even offer occasional updates. Your openness, accountability, and responsibility about finances build trust that will ensure confidence in any future financial decisions.

Bad Vibes: Parishioners Not Connecting Well with Each Other

Your parish is 100 percent people, and most will have a clear idea about their own situation in terms of racial, ethnic, gender, and economic class. If there has been any parish bias for or against any of the groups within your parish, then this problem needs your immediate attention and a process that you can begin right now toward a cure. Call on each group for expertise and advice on how to alter any parish policies that are promoting hurt or insensitivity or exacerbating tensions in these groups.

Pay close attention to such conflicts, but see them as an opportunity rather than a problem. This can be your greatest chance to make a huge difference for good right away, and it can have a far-reaching impact! Broken steel that is welded back together is actually stronger than the original piece. Customer service that fixes a problem for a customer creates a more loyal customer than if there had been no problem in the first place. Meet with everyone you can about the issue, and try to see common ground for a solution.

Bad Homilies: Not Speaking the Word of the Lord Well

This is a sensitive area since it reflects personally on the skill and talent of parish clergy. However, a spirit of humility can help here. No one ever finds success alone, so we all need mentors and wise coaches to help us learn valuable skills. Paul had Barnabas as a mentor. Mark had Peter. You can offer your clergy many internet sermon helps and even develop a small group that will review and help them in their delivery. Nothing helps more or creates faster change than watching a video of yourself speaking. For those with language barriers, there are many programs available to help.

Bad Staff Members: Stopping Good Work from Your Team

How will you handle toxic staff members? You will need to act, or you will be seen as ineffective by the healthy, productive people on your staff. Praise your staff publicly; offer your critical review of toxic members only privately. As toxic behavior often occurs behind the scenes, make public what the covert issues are if initial corrective intervention doesn't work. If your staff person is unmoved by your honest and helpful positive coaching, then that person must be let go. It will benefit the rest of the staff and the parish.

Malcontents

This is huge source of headaches for parish leaders! You may get emails or letters from very upset people. But how many people really know about the problem? Don't make malcontents famous by automatically responding in public to each one! See them in the overall context of parish needs. Your careful analysis of their comments may reveal a legitimate whistle-blower with something important to tell. Do not take critical comments personally, but look at them calmly and objectively. Still, recognize that comments may come from malcontents who aren't motivated by a desire to make your parish better, but by something other.

Nevertheless, be careful of your public comments, since reputations are at stake. Sometimes letting them speak out can reveal to others how out of balance they are. Stay calm, and do your job. Others will then compare you favorably with them. If malcontents are on parish committees and are resistant to any reasonable intervention, then you may need to remove them. Some people are simply *inconsolable*. No matter what you do, they will not be satisfied. Leave them alone with their misery, and do not let them distract you.

I was once assigned to a parish that was deeply split into factions. Before I arrived, the entire rectory staff had been removed for various acts of malfeasance. Half the parish felt victorious, and half felt they had lost valued ministers. Our new parish team decided not to make any big changes but rather to just do all the ordinary things really well. The priests also preached the Masses in weekly rotation, with one priest speaking at all weekend Masses. People could see the camaraderie we had, as each Mass had a celebrant and a preacher.

In another parish, our school was focused on cooperation among faculty, parents, and students. After much consultation, we developed a comprehensive educational plan involving input from school staff and parents for their student's welfare. We all did everything we could to help each group meet our goals for a solid Catholic education. Parents and school staff signed on to the agreement at the start of the school year. If anyone was not supportive or consistent with the goals that they had signed onto at the beginning of the year, then they had to be removed, whether student, parent, or teacher. Life works to the extent that we keep our agreements. Sometimes, unfortunately, students were removed because their parents could not support the school program of Catholic education that they had already agreed to. Sometimes it was the teacher, and sometimes it was the student. The overall goal of Catholic education remained paramount.

DISASTERS, MISTAKES, AND SCANDALS

Every parish will eventually encounter a crisis, whether a natural disaster, an unfortunate staff mistake, or a malicious act that causes scandal. These tend to be sudden events that take you by surprise. Fair enough. But having a disaster plan already in place can help when it is difficult to think clearly, especially if the media are asking questions and your parishioners also want to know what is going on. Remember that, in the absence of information, people tend to fill in the blanks. You do not want that!

Better to provide accurate information up front that prevents rumors and gossip from even starting. Getting in front of the story is paramount. You must stand before your community and demonstrate that you are taking care of business. The basic rule of public relations in crisis is to tell it all, tell it fast, and tell it accurately. Of course in legal cases, you must abide by the law as well. You should immediately contact your diocesan legal department for consultation on how to proceed. Any delay could make the situation worse or cause even more hurt. Your diocesan legal department will advise you on how to safeguard the rights of everyone involved.

This is your opportunity to address any loss of morale among your people. Remember the words of our Lord to St. Peter when our Lord knew his followers would be challenged: "You must strengthen your brothers" (Lk 22:32). People will know right away whether you are hiding information, obfuscating, or just not being truthful. Clarity is your way forward.

One example from my own ministry is our parish response when the clergy abuse and cover-up scandals first broke in 2002. I scheduled a town-hall-type meeting where parishioners could hear concise explanations about what was going on and ask all of their questions. Parishioners have a right to know what is happening in the Church and what is being done both to prevent further harm and to hold individuals responsible for harm they have done. I also reminded them that they must never let the bad example of other people affect their faith.

Another example is an effort I made as a pastor in an area of Los Angeles that had many brushfires and earthquakes. I provided a comprehensive document detailing emergency protocols. I also provided the entire staff with maps showing the locations of the parish's gas, water, and power shutoffs and a list of vendors, plumbers, and electricians to call in emergencies.

LEADING YOURSELF

Before you can hope to lead others, you have to lead yourself and have control of your thoughts and emotions. The last chapter urged you to connect with your own narrative to discover what feeds you. How do you feel about exercising authority and making hard decisions: saying no or yes to different requests? How have you experienced and reacted to authority in the past? Let your love for your people inspire you with courage to face these questions and seek honest answers, which will make you a better person, a more effective minister, and a successful leader. These are some areas in which parish leaders may struggle.

Procrastination

Do nothing about your procrastination at first! Just think intentionally about the project or task you are avoiding. This will prevent you from distracting yourself with "busy work" instead of doing the real work that needs to be done. Break large tasks into smaller units that are easier to complete quickly and successfully, and complete one small task toward the overall goal each day. Each task done gives a quick and welcome sense of success. As small as it is, you realize you are doing something!

Resistance to Review

People do not like to be told what to do. God actually designed us to resist it. However, we eagerly seek another's wise opinion if we feel it is in our best interests. Athletes appreciate the advice of a wise and kindly coach who helps them correct mistakes and so better achieve their goals in their sport. If you are making mistakes that seriously undermine your effectiveness, don't you want to know what they are? Of course, you likely only want guidance from others who share your goals.

Not Being a Good and Kindly Coach

Nothing can kill staff motivation like a leader who does not respect them or help them grow. If your people believe you are on their side and want to help them be successful and reach their goals, they will listen to anything you have to say. If you signal that you do not have their best interests in mind, you will have an inactive and apathetic staff. Again, athletes carefully listen to their coaches since they believe their advice will help them make more free throws, touchdowns, or home runs! A good coach may prescribe tough medicine that is necessary for good performance. What are the characteristics of a good and kindly coach? He or she first says peace; signals respect, patience, and clarity of purpose; knows the goal; and can offer clear direction about how to get there.

If your professional and volunteer staff members are afraid of making mistakes, they will venture nothing. Let them know that taking a risk and making mistakes is okay if the intentions are good. Zero tolerance of mistakes freezes your staff into doing nothing out of that very fear of mistakes. Let them know that all of their remarks at meetings are welcome.

Disrespecting Staff

Safeguard the dignity of persons even as you might disagree over policy. Never humiliate, mock, or shame in the interest of winning an argument. People who mock others align themselves with the Romans, who used crucifixion precisely for its humiliating effect. Shouting, mocking, and similar tactics add an emotional attack that overpowers any logic or reasonable argument. Your opponent responds only to the emotional attack and not to your logic or reason.

CURING YOURSELF

You cannot cure anything or anyone else without first curing yourself, which means tending to what is unhealthy in your behaviors, emotions, attitudes, and character. You must become a good manager of all these different aspects of your life. You are right up front for everyone to see, warts and all. Your personality is highly visible, so take care to take care of it. It will be on display as people see how you respond to requests, criticisms, complaints, or even compliments. Any those could pull you off focus and change your attitude for the worse. Not much good happens after that!

Your life can become quite hectic soon after your arrival. Choose and use a word or phrase that reminds you of your mission—who you are and what you are to do today, this week, this month, this year, and with your life. I use the simple phrase *Alter Christus*, or "another Christ." It reminds me to be the person of

Christ in every conversation and event. The following are some other ways you can take care of yourself.

Work Continuously to Improve Your Energy

Jesus asks us to "Follow him" as disciples to bring the kingdom of God to the world. We will look at that in more detail in the next chapter. However, we know he wants us to follow him with our whole body, heart, soul, and mind. You must dedicate everything that you are and have to this mission.

- *Physical energy.* Your body and your mind are intimately connected, so take good care of your body. Make sure you pay attention to the amount of sleep you get, the nutrition you consume, and the exercise you do. These are not luxuries but requirements based on the way God designed your body. Make a late-evening "to-do" list for the next day; your mind will then know you are taking care of business and not keep you awake with thoughts and worries.

- *Emotional energy.* What triggers your anger, anxiety, fear, love, laughter, and joy? What kind of people do you find interesting? Draining? What activities do you find relaxing and rejuvenating? Knowing the answers to these questions and keeping them in mind will help you not to be surprised, lose your temper, or jump to conclusions when you encounter these triggers.

- *Mental energy.* When are you most alert? When are you most disconnected from your surroundings? What events do you find most interesting? Exciting? Draining? Do you set aside time to learn, study, and grow in knowledge of your faith, or do you use all that energy on other matters? If not your faith, why not? Do you have good self-awareness? Take some time to answer these questions. What do they reveal about your priorities? Decide today to dedicate time to growing in your knowledge of our faith, whether from books or even appropriate YouTube channels.

- *Spiritual energy.* What forms of spiritual practice are best for you? Studying or meditating on scripture, contemplative prayer, devotions such as the Rosary or Stations of the Cross, belonging to a prayer and faith-sharing small group, sacramental celebrations, retreats? All are useful; figure out which are most rewarding for you.

Pay Attention to Where You Spend Your Time

Focus on events with the biggest bang for the buck. Let perspective and context guide the choices you make about daily activity and schedules. Sunday Mass is certainly the most important weekly event. Every action must advance the mission that you initially set. Prioritize your behavior according to those goals.

Do Not Let Yourself Succumb to Self-Doubt

In the movie *The Passion of the Christ*, the devil tempts Jesus with self-doubt about the possibility of saving the whole world, saying, "It is too much for one man." Fear and doubt start with self-consciousness. You ask, "How am I doing? How will I do?" That self-consciousness can slowly erode your ability to lead great projects effectively, as you will be more focused on your own reputation than on project progress. Focus instead on your love for your parishioners and your desire to offer the goodness of our faith to them. Step back and ask, "What is this parish event, big wedding, important meeting, long-awaited talk, or building project really about?" Remember the original mission or purpose of events like these, which is simply to make the love of God present.

Remember That Parish Success Is Not about You!

The attention you receive as a parish leader can inadvertently feed your ego in a bad way. Always remember that you are about Jesus, *his* mission, and *his* way of accomplishing that mission. Put your personal preferences aside for now. Focus on first things first. How do you feel about criticism or negative comments or pressure to do things? Do you brood over them? Do you remember only the negative and forget the positive? It is good to reflect on how you react to both negative and positive comments. Do you collapse with the negative or get a big head with the positive? Jesus would often be greatly praised in one town for miracles performed and be almost stoned in another for the same miracles. Yet he remained the same in both, for he sought to please only his heavenly Father. That is what kept him on an even keel in both places.

Never Be Disillusioned by the Sinfulness of Others

Check your illusions at the parish door. Recognize that people can be great sinners and also great saints. You meet both, a lot! Often in the same person. So do not be shocked at evil behavior or surprised by good behavior. Both are in abundant supply. There was a time when the Church consisted entirely of just a handful of people surrounded by a massive, corrupt, and evil Roman Empire. The disciples learned to never let another's lack of faith, hope, or love affect their own faith, hope, and love. Your confidence comes from these same virtues. Confidence means you have an assurance about how you handle any situation. *Confidence* comes from two Latin words strung helpfully together: *con-fidere*, meaning "with faith" or "with trust."

I was once assigned to a very difficult pastor. After one year, the other associate pastor left the priesthood because he was so disillusioned. A year after that, another associate left for the same reason! The archdiocese soon sent a priest to tell me that I could leave this parish and go to any other parish I wanted. Well, I simply said no. Why would I allow a pastor like that to affect me? I was there to change him! I stayed but, alas, had no effect on him whatsoever! Nevertheless, I did not allow him to affect me. I had learned never to let another's lack of faith, hope, or love shake my own my faith, hope, and love.

While I was serving in another parish, I had three back-to-back appointments one evening. It was going to be a busy evening. However, one by one during the day each of them called to cancel, all of course with good reasons. I was relieved at first and happy to have the evening free but then slowly became somewhat chagrined at my response. Why was I happy that I would *not* be meeting these people? Would I be happier if no one ever came in? Was I looking at these appointments as a burden or an opportunity to help change lives for the better? I knew I needed to reframe how I viewed my time or face a lifetime of resenting people ever coming to see me.

Thinking about the ongoing need to remind yourself what your time is for leads us to the lessons of chapter 4 and the highly important reason why you do what you do!

KEY TAKEAWAYS

- You can cure some problems shortly after assuming your new role.
- The Luke 10 Leadership directive to cure the sick is where you make your first decisions.
- Choose the right problems to solve.
- Your cures for parish problems are where your people will first come to know your leadership skills and style.
- Make sure you have cured yourself.

4.
ANNOUNCE THE KINGDOM OF GOD

"Say to them, 'The kingdom of God is at hand for you.'"

—Luke 10:9b

KEY IDEAS

Things change dramatically at this point. This is when you will announce the kingdom of God and invite people to join it publicly. So far, the first three steps from our Lord in Luke 10 Leadership have been about you: your words and your behavior, how you have come in peace, patiently learned the local culture, and started to set things right. Now you will call on people to publicly change their words and behavior; you will invite them to turn in a new direction and follow Jesus, who personifies the kingdom of God. This is the time you proclaim just "how things are done" in the kingdom of God: we follow our Lord and his Church.

Christ is the one who makes the kingdom come alive for each person. Your purpose now is to help your people encounter Christ in personal and life-changing ways. You can use every manner of human communication, personal connection, social media, and whatever else helps to authentically reveal the kingdom of God.

Announcing the kingdom demands from you both leadership skills and the courage to speak this bold and life-changing invitation. You are now actively engaged in leading other people's lives, and your courage will come from Jesus himself. When people see that you share their challenges, their joys and sorrows, their worries and pain—and still can help them find hope, they will follow you. When people see that you have come in peace, learned their culture, and help them in practical ways, they will follow you. When people see that you love them, they will follow you.

A leader shows his or her people a way of true happiness that they will want for themselves! Show your staff and parishioners the destination of lasting happiness, which is the kingdom of God, and let them develop the way to get there. Show that you trust them, and they will rise to the occasion, as happened with our Lord and his disciples.

What has happened so far in your Luke 10 Leadership process? Your people have benefited from your presence with them and have received a lot from you. You have come in peace, you have learned their local culture and understand "how things are done here," and you have wonderfully solved some practical problems for your people. All well and good, but not ultimately why our Lord sent you to this parish. It is now time for you to request something of your people.

Jesus asks you to announce the kingdom of God. What does that mean? It means that you will invite people to live "how things are done" in the kingdom of God. This invitation to conversion requires you to ask people to change the way they have done things in the past and move toward following the way of our Lord. This where you ask your people to buy into the kingdom of God. Above all, announcing the kingdom of God means asking people to change their lives! You will actually be asking people to return to the way they were originally made to live.

WHAT IS THE KINGDOM OF GOD?

The best way to comprehend the kingdom of God is to know the person, words, and deeds of Jesus. The first words Jesus spoke when he began his ministry could not have been more simple or direct. While walking along the shore of the Sea of Galilee, he came across ordinary fishermen at work. Jesus approached each one, looked at him directly, and simply said, "Follow me!" In the ancient world, following meant more than casual imitation. Rather, following another meant something more like *incorporating* that person's life into your own. It was a complete reorientation of one's life path. Followers became one with their leader.

A Pharisee once asked Jesus which commandment was the most important. Our Lord responded by revealing the kingdom of God with a clear and compelling threefold command: love God, love others, and love yourself (see Matthew 22:34–40). Jesus asks that you love as he loves. So what is love? Love is willing the authentic good of another. Our Lord commands you to take hold of your life—who you are and what you have to give—and then do everything within your power to use yourself and your gifts to deepen your love for God and enable the authentic good of the other and yourself. You love the people you serve and work with and want the best for them as God designed. This will enable their lasting happiness. We believe the kingdom of God will provide that lasting happiness both in the life to come but also in this life. The kingdom of God is not so much about wealth or health or any new parish program, but about the profound happiness that comes from living the life of love that Jesus himself lived.

Jesus lived this special kingdom-of-God love even on the Cross. Remember the powerful words he said there: "Father, forgive them, they know not what they do" (Lk 23:34). "Amen, I say to you, today you will be with me in Paradise" (Lk 23:43). "'Woman, behold, your son.' Then he said to the disciple, 'Behold, your mother'" (Jn 19:26–27). Even as he endured the agony of crucifixion, Jesus expressed only love, even toward his executioners! The kingdom of God is about this profound and enduring love.

THE KINGDOM MUST BE ANNOUNCED IN EVERY AGE AND EVERY CULTURE

We believe God created human persons in love, to live on earth with love for each other—this is what living the kingdom of God means. The kingdom of God began much earlier than any civilization, culture, or age. The kingdom of God is not Western or Eastern, European or American, but rather it is universal. So why is announcing this kingdom still so necessary? Why does it still seem like such a new thing?

This fourth step of Luke 10 Leadership, announcing the kingdom of God, begs the question of why people are in need of this message in the first place. Why did Jesus feel the need to send out seventy-two disciples with all this special training? Why was the pagan world so problematic? What did people need saving *from*? Clearly the world had become a very sinful and violent place, but how did the world get that way? Why would human beings ever seek to harm others? Where does that evil impulse come from? We need to look at the creation accounts in Genesis, the very first book in the Bible, which contain the very first revelations of the kingdom of God.

The Kingdom of God First Revealed

The story of Adam and Eve is profoundly important and deeply meaningful for you, who are called to leadership in the Church.

It has many aspects that surface in contemporary debates about evolution and science (our Catholic faith affirms that there is never a contradiction between faith and science). However, our focus here is only on that part of the creation accounts that describes the origin of the first sin, which amazingly happened in a beautiful garden that God himself designed!

God places Adam and Eve in a garden. It is a testament to his love for them that he gives them a beautiful and harmonious place in which to live. He created them in love to love each other and to enjoy multiplying as well. Adam recognizes Eve as "bone of my bones and flesh of my flesh" (Gn 2:23), meaning that man and woman are perfectly equal in dignity to each other. They are also famously "naked" because they are fully open and transparent to each other.

The Kingdom Lost through Sin

In the garden, God's declaration of the tree of the knowledge of good and evil as off-limits to Adam and Eve is no arbitrary line in the sand that God sets up as some kind of test. God does not play games with the people he created and deeply loves. What the declaration means is that only God can decide what is right and wrong. You should be grateful for that! If humans could decide what is right and wrong, people could walk into your home at any time of the day and take something from you simply because they decided it was good for them. How could you argue against that? If each person selfishly decided what is right and wrong for him or herself, then your burglar would have every right to take your stuff. Moreover, if that burglar were bigger than you, then you would never get your stuff back. We would end up living by the code of might makes right.

When people took upon themselves the power to decide good and evil, then might did become right. In fact, directly after Adam and Eve's story comes the story of Cain, who selfishly murders his own brother Abel because he wants to retaliate after a perceived slight by his brother. When people replace God with their own desires, then those desires are what they worship. Nothing good can come from that!

Changing our human nature from love to selfish dominance over others is the first sin, the original sin. That sin predisposes us to take from others rather than give of ourselves to them. All sins are some form of the original sin of selfishness: instead of following God's design for love, we follow our own plan for selfish gain. Sin actually changes our God-given loving nature into something selfish instead.

Notice that God's first words to Adam and Eve after their sin are "Where are you?" It is not that God does know geographically where these people are. Rather, he is asking after deeper things: "Where are the people I made? I made you to be loving helpmates to each other. You have made yourselves into something else. You will only find unhappiness with your selfish choices. The normal work of caring for the garden, which before your sin you found meaningful and fulfilling because it was done out of love will now become meaningless and painful, since you will not be working to help each other." Adam and Eve become estranged. They even put on clothes since they were no longer united as one in perfect love and transparency to each other.

The Restoration of the Kingdom

St. Paul, an esteemed scholar of the Jewish scriptures, recognized Jesus as the New Adam (see Romans 5:12–21). Jesus lived the life that Adam was supposed to live but did not. Mary is the New Eve because by bearing the Savior of the world she cooperated in the reversal of Eve's act of selfishness. The kingdom of God is our Lord's mission to restore the original creation of human beings, first in himself and then in his Church.

MEETING JESUS MAKES
THE KINGDOM OF GOD
HAPPEN ANEW

Almost every story in the gospels involves Jesus meeting people in need, especially those who have fallen victim to the violence and suffering of the world, now rampant and widespread since the sin of Adam and Eve. The people Jesus encounters are looking to him to make a difference. Every meeting results in some transformation, usually for the better. You cannot meet the Lord and stay the same. In fact, any change for the better in your life is the sign that the meeting actually happened. Our lives find purpose, meaning, and fulfillment from encountering Christ. We share the joy we have found so that others may find joy that is complete and life that is abundant (see John 10:10, 15:11).

While those who received miracles upon meeting Jesus were happy, not everyone was cured. Our Lord intended a deeper happiness and fulfillment that goes way beyond healing of any physical sickness. For example, returning to the story of Peter's mother-in-law at Capernaum, which we explored briefly in the last chapter, news quickly spreads to the whole town of the healing. Soon, crowds show up at Peter's door looking to have their own situations healed. After a while, Jesus leaves to pray at a nearby mountain. The crowds eventually find him and beg him to return because there are still people waiting to meet him and hoping for healing. Amazingly, Jesus says he will move on to other towns to "proclaim the good news of the kingdom of God, because for this purpose I have been sent" (Lk 4:43).

You Need to Meet Jesus First

If a cure will help you love more, then, God willing, you will receive a cure. If God believes that facing your illness with courage and hope will help you love more, then your sickness is God's calling to you to live that deeper love. Love changes suffering. People will work at an extremely difficult job because of their love for their family and their deep desire to provide for them. Parents will sacrifice their own luxuries to provide for their kids. Love changes everything.

Your joy—no matter what is going on in your life, whether health, wealth, suffering, or sickness—comes from the profound experience of being loved by God. Our God sent his Son to come into the world in peace, help you live your life fully, cure what ails you, and bring the love of the Father to you. This is Luke 10 Leadership directly from our heavenly Father!

Your Purpose Is to Help Others Encounter Jesus

In every gospel story where Jesus meets someone in need, the person's life is changed amazingly for the better, even if some do not recognize it right away. Every good thing happens when you meet the Lord. Your mission in your parish—in every activity, in every moment of the day, in every conversation and meeting, and especially during the liturgy—is to help make an authentic meeting with our Lord happen for the people you work with and for. This is the *why* of everything you do all day long. At every moment of the day, you should be able to say immediately that you are doing whatever you are doing to enable your people to meet Jesus. Every member of your staff and hopefully every parishioner should be able to say the same. This is a key way you can measure your success as a parish leader. If you walk up to any parishioner and ask, "Why are you a Catholic?" or "What do you do here in this parish?" the answer should simply be "I meet Jesus every day, and I help other people meet Jesus!"

I once asked a parishioner who worked at an airplane assembly factory what he did there. I expected an answer like "I assemble the aircraft wings" or "I work on the engines." Instead, he replied, "I reunite families at Thanksgiving!" He saw the larger context and higher purpose of his work in a noble and meaningful way.

Actions are meaningful when they are related to a larger context or perspective, and there is no larger context or perspective than meeting the Lord, which puts your eternal life into play. Anything you do that helps your people have that authentic encounter is the most meaningful thing you will ever do.

A Person, Not a Program

Today there are thousands of programs, retreats, speakers, seminars, podcasts, webinars, and other well-thought-out and useful opportunities that promise this or that amazing result of renewed parishioner participation. It is well and good that people are thinking creatively about evangelization, and I encourage your research into these tools for possible use in your parish. But the kingdom of God is about persons rather than programs. The first person is, of course, Christ Jesus. And the next person to consider is *you*. Announcing the kingdom of God in your parish or ministry is all about you and the kind of person you are.

People do not follow causes as much as they follow people they know and respect who have causes. Your people will want to see that you have kingdom-of-God love deep in your heart. They will want to see that the person of Jesus is at the center of your life. When Jesus called his first disciples to follow him, they had no idea what he was talking about, yet they followed because they knew him and trusted him. They had lived with Jesus for years in the village of Capernaum and had come to know that he came in peace, took the time to know them, and sought to cure problems in practical ways.

In the first century, there were only the stories and lessons of Jesus. There were no churches, parishes, programs, retreats, seminars, or promotions. There were only people who followed leaders who followed Jesus with all of their heart and all of their strength. That made all the difference—so much so such that within a few generations, much of the Roman Empire had become Christian.

Jesus means for that same dynamic to happen today with you as a parish leader. Be the person whom people will want to follow. Be the person who others know has their very best interests at heart. Be the person who brings the person of Jesus to everyone you meet—at every parish event, in every parish conversation, and, if you are a priest, especially at every parish liturgy.

PRIESTS HAVE A UNIQUE ROLE IN ANNOUNCING THE KINGDOM OF GOD

Priests act in the person of Christ (*in persona Christi*) to bring about the kingdom of God (see CCC, 1547–1568). A very important image used in scripture to depict the relationship of Christ to his Church is that of a groom's relationship to his bride. People willing to give their lives to each other in marriage clearly want what is best for their spouse. Remember that the story of Adam and Eve is also the story of a marriage. Jesus is the New Adam who meets his bride, the Church. In the story of the wedding feast at Cana, Jesus acts as the groom in ensuring that there is enough wine for the celebration to last. He wants what he knows will help bring the couple lasting happiness in their marriage.

Just as Jesus did, priests gather people together into a church, a community of love and service to others (see CCC, 541). That loving community may be the beginning of your people's experience of Jesus and the kingdom of God. Every parish event and especially every Mass should deepen that experience. The unique roles of priests as confessors and as presiders at the eucharistic liturgy expressly unite people into a community that repents of any selfishness in the Sacrament of Penance and Reconciliation and renews the commitment to love each other at every Mass. In both events, the priest celebrant is the person in whom people expect they will meet the Lord in a unique and fundamental way. This is the priest's role even if we priests are weak and/or lack talent for speaking or organizational abilities (see CCC, 1550).

The Essential Role of a Pastor

If you are a pastor, you should of course take yourself, your personal faith development, and parish leadership seriously. You should never delegate away or minimize your role as the person at the top or center of the organizational chart. Peter was given the keys to the kingdom, and the Twelve were appointed leaders. As a priest you share in their leadership role, and your calling was designed by our Lord for a specific purpose.

Make sure you know what your role is in a Catholic parish. Since you stand in the person of Christ and as the Bridegroom, your main qualities should be those of . . . a good husband. Wives rarely choose their husbands because they are good speakers or can organize a great meeting. They seek a husband who is faithful, loyal, hard-working, courageous, and open to creating new life in a family. Your parish, the Bride of Christ, is looking for those same qualities in you. Your model is the person of Jesus.

Great authority lies with the pastor. It is almost impossible to lead any change in a Catholic parish without the pastor's buy-in; change always starts or ends at the top. Remember that the power you have is the power to do something good for the kingdom of God. Your power as pastor is your opportunity to bring people to Jesus. It is not about a title or an award meant to puff up your ego.

Do not let anything get in the way of your God-given task to do the good you have been called to do. You cannot delegate this power. You should never hide behind parish councils, committees, canon laws, or staff decisions. You have been called to lead, so take the call seriously. Collaboration and delegation cannot lessen your responsibility.

People will follow you if they see the person of Christ in you. Maybe you have great speaking skills, or maybe you don't. Maybe you can run a great meeting, or maybe not. If you love your people, they will see the person of Jesus in you and follow, trusting you will lead them to Christ.

ANNOUNCING THE KINGDOM IN A HOSTILE CULTURE

Catholic thinking about the kingdom of God is based on an image of nuptial love where the bridegroom and we, the Church, are the bride. This image becomes especially meaningful when you look at wedding vows. The soon-to-be spouses promise love in good times and in bad, in sickness and in health, all the days of their lives. This vow reflects the everlasting love—love, no matter what—Christ promises for you.

Husbands and Wives Proclaim the Kingdom of God!

I have celebrated over a thousand weddings in more than forty years as a priest. I can attest that at every one of those weddings I have seen guests become misty-eyed when the bride and groom recite their vows. The kind of commitment they promise is sadly becoming rarer these days, and so it is deeply meaningful to witness it. Couples promise that there will be love, no matter what! They also promise to restore their vows whenever they are damaged or even broken. That is their commitment.

When your spouse gets the flu, do you now say the marriage is over? Of course not! Your love is not based on health or wealth or some program guaranteeing success, but on a commitment to offer your life for the happiness of another. Every marriage is a series of stops and starts as couples negotiate the many challenges in their life together. Even following the most serious of breaks, like infidelity, those couples who know how to recover their love are the happiest of all. Married couples also promise to be open to the possibility of new life. In that, they share in the creative power of God. This is not a small thing. To bring new life into the world is the ultimate commitment to the future.

In the kingdom of God, we celebrate authentic love wherever it is and are very happy when people love each other, but we understand marriage as a specific relationship involving one man and one woman that is especially oriented to the possibility of new life and toward the loving unity of that man and woman. Today, same-sex couples seek this same union of marriage. This is currently an area of hot debate that you will certainly encounter in your parish if you haven't already.

You may think it impossible to announce this part of the kingdom of God. However, if people challenge you on the requirement of one man and one woman, you might ask if there is any relationship that they would *not* accept? After all, there are many ways that people can possibly form relationships, such as three or more people marrying together, or parents marrying their children, or even brothers and sisters marrying each other. If, as Adam and Eve believed, we can each decide what is right and wrong, what basis is there for denying any of these relationships?

During one of my parish assignments, a same-sex couple asked if they could enroll their adopted child into our parish school. I told them that their child was welcome, but that, as a Catholic school, we would teach all of our students the Catholic understanding of marriage. I am glad they enrolled the child! Many of our school parents are in irregular marriages, are living together before marriage, or harbor other sinful situations such as untreated addictions. We seek to help these parishioners in any way we can and do not handicap their children because of their parents' unresolved sin. But we certainly don't shy away from handing on what the Church has long taught as revealed to us from our Lord.

Proclaim and Speak Out Boldly

Never dilute or minimize what you ask of your people. You must announce the kingdom as Jesus spoke and lived it: always with love and respect, yet ever faithful to the tradition of the Church, which we received from Christ and which has been authentically transmitted through the centuries by the teaching authority first given to the apostles. People will respect your courage if it is connected with compassion. Never try to align the kingdom of God with what focus groups say they want or what you think people might want to hear. Your message does not *follow* people, but *leads* them to the Lord! Say and do what you believe. You should be able to describe in detail "how things are done" in the kingdom of God.

The kingdom of God is also localized in a geographical place. It is meant to be modeled not only in your parish, but also wherever your parishioners are . . . at school, at work, or at home. You invite people to live in this place of love wherever they are.

THE KINGDOM OFFERS LASTING HAPPINESS TO ALL

Chapter 2 revealed how the Romans were amazed that the early Christians truly cared for people outside of their own families. Christians seemed to care for people just because they were in need, and they expected nothing in return. In the same way, invite people to join your parish, volunteer in ministries, or simply contribute—not to make your parish bigger and better, but because you believe that these activities are good for them in their own spiritual journeys and as such will further the kingdom of God.

The Kingdom of God Is for Everyone

Christians were the first religion to seek converts. No other ancient religion ever sought converts: not the Assyrians, Persians, Babylonians, Greeks, or Romans. They would, of course, accept converts since it helped their empire become bigger and stronger. However, Christians had no empire. They sought only to share the person of Jesus and the kingdom he proclaimed because only this would bring true happiness to individuals and peace to the world. Christians did everything out of love, and their neighbors were amazed that nothing would distract them from their love.

God's plan for us is rooted deeply in the way he designed us. While we often think that personal success is the best plan, eventually we discover that although personal success is rewarding, it is often not fulfilling. We soon discover that helping our community succeed draws us much closer to being the truly happy and fulfilled people God has created us to be. Consider the woman at the well in John 4:4–42. She came back again and again for more water for herself. But seeking power, pleasure, and wealth for oneself alone is never enough. Jesus instead promised her the Living Water, which is the love we have for others that is never emptied. The success we most seek is lasting happiness—eternal life—for ourselves and for those around us.

You should seek that lasting happiness not only for those people in your ministry but for the larger community around you and even across the planet. Think about how your parish or ministry can ally itself with some of the larger social justice efforts of your diocese. How can you help bring the kingdom of God far beyond your parish boundaries? How especially meaningful that work will be for the people you lead!

Toward the end of his career, Otto Kernberg, one of the most famous psychiatrists of our time, brought his lifetime of insight to the analysis of organizations. He famously wrote that an unhealthy organization can soon make healthy people sick, while an organization that is healthy will soon make even unhealthy people well. Basically, you become the organization you join. If your parish is healthy and lives the values and truth of the kingdom of God, then unhealthy people will find a cure for their problems within it. If your parish does not live kingdom values, then even healthy people will soon become sick there. Kernberg affirms that your parish or your ministry can be the source of profound healing for those who most need it.

The Kingdom of God Is a Moral Place

Jesus came to offer a life that will bring profound happiness to those who follow him. It is wise to present the Church's moral teachings in light of this ultimate goal. You will be happier if you do not lie, steal, or murder. You will be happier if you keep your promises and commitments in marriage. In short, you will be happier if you live in the way that God designed you to live. Two verses you should memorize that affirm this idea are John 10:10, "I came so that they might have life and have it more abundantly," and John 15:11, "I have told you this so that my joy may be in you and your joy may be complete." Our moral guidelines are not simply institutional rules such as many other organizations might have. Following Christ in all things means that we live as God made us to live and so, being united to God and one another in love, find the lasting happiness that he wants for us. When you operate according to your manufacturer's instructions, everything works out well!

JESUS EMBODIED AND PRACTICED LUKE 10 LEADERSHIP

When Jesus was born in Bethlehem, the angels sang of peace, signaling to those who would hear that the child intended no harm, only good. He lived among us, sharing our food and our human life. No one can say that he did not take the time to learn about the human condition or the culture in which he lived, preached, and healed. Jesus cured the sick and performed miracles that immediately helped people with practical problems. Lastly, he announced that the kingdom of God was at hand.

Jesus called people to leave their former lives and follow him. He expected specific behaviors from his followers. He calls us to turn our lives around, repent, and walk in his footsteps. Yet he always respects our freedom. When a rich man asks him how to go to heaven (see Mark 10:17), Jesus explains it all quite clearly. The young man listens carefully, but turns away. Jesus respects his decision and does not run after him. Was Jesus uncaring? Hardly! Was he forgetful of the parable of the lost sheep? Not at all. That parable describes a sheep that is lost and the shepherd runs after it.

This rich young man just had everything clearly explained to him by the master teacher, Jesus, and so is not lost. He walks away, and our Lord respects his freely considered decision.

Some scripture scholars think that the rich man in this Gospel of Mark was actually Mark himself. They believe that he eventually repented, returned to our Lord, and later related his own story in his gospel account to affirm the power of the invitation of Jesus to follow him. Mark's change of his life to follow Jesus has made a difference for all who have read his gospel over the centuries.

Jesus never diluted or downgraded his message about the kingdom of God in order to attract followers. He called people to follow him and accept life in the kingdom. Period. He offers his message about the Eucharist in John 6:22–71, teaching that we are called to consume his Body and Blood. Many in the crowd turn away. Does he run after them? Does he shout "Come back! It's only a symbol!" Not at all. In verse 67, Jesus turns to his disciples and quietly asks, "Do you also want to leave?" They wonderfully respond that they will stay because they know he has the words of eternal life.

NEW METHODS OF EVANGELIZING

While the message of Jesus remains the same, how we present it can and should change to meet the way people think about and understand their lives in every time and place. If you want your people to encounter Jesus, to truly meet Christ, you must adapt your delivery of the Good News to fit their culture. After all, what worked in the Middle Ages or even ten years ago might not work well today; even what worked last year may now seem outdated. The message of love always remains at the center of announcing the kingdom of God, but you must be creative, innovative, and clever in how you present it for the world you live in right now. St. John Paul II encouraged Catholics to use new methods that draw upon the original ardor, energy, and spirit of the first generation of disciples. Some of his ideas follow.

Social Media

Constant access to social media and other sources of information is a key marker of contemporary culture. You cannot escape it and still remain engaged with your parish and your parishioners. One obvious driving force behind the explosion of social media platforms is instant connection to people you may otherwise engage only rarely or never at all. Admittedly, the internet lends itself quite easily to unleashing the worst in human nature. The quasi-anonymous nature of posting and commenting can lead people to offer only their worst emotional expressions and half-considered opinions without any pressure to present substantive reasons for them.

It is a tricky business to learn to navigate the complicated world of social media—and cyberspace in general—responsibly and wisely to better your community and the world. But fortunately there are many hints and guides to help you, and I urge you to investigate some of these if you haven't already. At the very least, always keep in mind that you are connecting with real human persons; be respectful in your comments, and realize that any comments you receive are also from real human persons. Remember also that what you post is likely to be seen by more people than those with whom you are intending to communicate, and so always ask yourself if you mind that what you are posting is public. If you do, communicate by phone call, direct individual text message, confidential email, or an actual old-time face-to-face conversation instead.

You should also consider having on your parish staff a competent tech person who understands social media well. No need for you to master it if you can rely on a trusted staff person to convey your messages and responses effectively. This position might even lend itself to a service-learning placement for an older high school student or a college student.

Our Lord meant for the kingdom of God to spread through real, person-to-person contact. You might think of social media as a kind of pre-evangelization event for connecting the people in your social media networks with their local parish, where they will mix with real people in a real community of persons. The kingdom of God is a real place with real people.

LEADERSHIP INSIGHTS FROM OUTSIDE THE CHURCH

There are other institutions, such as the business world and the military, that seek to motivate people today. Often you can recognize in them the leadership lessons from Luke 10. Church people tend not to look to the business world or the military for inspiration or wisdom about leadership, yet these institutions can offer you some wonderful insights.

Business

We can certainly find the basic steps of Luke 10 leadership operating within successful business models, particularly in efforts to motivate consumers to purchase things or buy into ideas. Remember that a business is created to make a product or a service that solves a problem. Entrepreneurs want to cure a problem with an affordable solution and so must understand the culture of their customers, just as you must understand the culture of your parish. Thomas Edison realized that gas lights were dangerous, dirty, and labor-intensive, so he developed a way to mass-produce safer and more reliable electric lighting that people would buy into.

Remember that thousands of your parishioners come together each day in various companies to work cooperatively to produce some good or service. Never denigrate what they are doing; rather, notice how these enterprises motivate people with the same steps that Jesus used. Observe, for example, advertising built on the personal endorsement of an admired celebrity, cultural leader, or a character who appeals to most people as a trustworthy person living a life most of us want. Business leaders know that people want to identify with attractive people doing things that we want to do and having things we want to have. Business leaders know the power of person-to-person contact. And we know that the kingdom of God is spread from person to person.

The Military

Every day, the military motivates thousands of young men and women to join the army, navy, air force, coast guard, or marines. These young men and women know they will undergo many months of rigorous training building up to a mission that may well lead to severe injury or even death. Yet the military always enjoys high enlistment. Never denigrate what they are doing. The basic military charge to every leader is "take care of your people and accomplish the mission." How simple and effective is that? It is essentially the same directive Jesus gave the seventy-two in Luke 10.

The military, like the Church, inspires people with the heroic lives of real people. The number one way the military inspires follower is by showcasing heroes. They honor men and women who have given their utmost effort to accomplish their missions—some having sacrificed their lives—just as the Church presents the lives of the saints and martyrs who have done the same.

THE COURAGE TO LEAD

Luke 10 begins with Jesus sending his disciples into dangerous territory. Jesus calls us to a life of courage and adventure, not safety. Your love for your people will summon the courage you need to call them to join the kingdom of God. Courage is a virtue that we often learn or "catch" from someone else, as we might catch another's enthusiasm. Courage is contagious, and it will slowly spread, taking root in those around you.

You might be inspired to courage by a war hero or one of the martyrs of the Church who faced a challenge directly. Courage can also come from within as you act to defend a loved one from sudden danger. When surrounded by hostile pagans, our ancestors in the faith drew courage from their love for one another, the example of Jesus, and stories of early saints and martyrs.

When I think about courage, I often recall a parishioner I knew who had been nominated for our school board. I thought she was too shy and quiet to be an effective voice. But at a quite large gathering of parents, she came to the microphone and delivered an amazingly eloquent and passionate speech. Where did she get the courage? She was advocating on behalf of her children. Love fuels courage, courage creates leaders, and leaders create followers.

What Is a Parish Leader?

First and foremost, leaders *create followers*. Having a brilliant message is not enough if no one wants to follow you. Leaders must reveal a new place where people want to go. People sense that the place where you lead them will make their lives happier, more meaningful, and more fulfilling. We believe the kingdom of God is that place. Leaders in the kingdom help people fulfill their mission as disciples of Jesus to bring the Good News of salvation to all whom they meet. As a parish leader, you commit to accomplishing the mission of our Lord to announce the kingdom of God; and you commit to caring for the people you lead because you love them and want them also to take up the call of discipleship, spreading the Good News.

Luke 10 reveals that leadership is a learnable behavior. Follow the Luke 10 Leadership steps: first say peace; eat what is set before you; cure the sick; announce the kingdom of God. This process is based on universal human dynamics and has been effective across many cultures for two thousand years.

Why Should People Follow You?

Your people are understandably focused on the immediate tasks of their everyday lives. They have family and other loved ones to care for and enjoy time with, professional responsibilities, homes to keep, and an array of other daily matters that occupy their time and attention. If they see that you can help them find happiness or solutions to their struggles and stresses, they will follow you. If they see in you a glimpse of the kingdom of God—which is where they want to be—they will follow you. The fishermen who met Jesus on the shores of the Sea of Galilee did not know or understand the mission of Jesus, but they believed he was a person who had their best interests at heart and could somehow fulfill their needs. They recognized that he came in peace, learned about and shared in their lives, and sought to make their lives better. They saw in him the kingdom of God, and they followed him.

Set aside any stereotypes you might have of leadership. Leadership is not shouting orders or dominating people. It is more than managing. It has nothing to do with extroversion or introversion. It simply means that people see that you care for them and that you have something good to offer them for their lasting happiness. It means showing your people what living in the kingdom of God looks like and helping them make their way there.

KEY TAKEAWAYS

- Now is when you call people to change their lives to follow Christ.
- The kingdom is about a person, not a program.
- This kingdom must be announced in every age and culture.
- Jesus came to restore the first kingdom in the garden.
- The kingdom of God lives the morality of Jesus.
- Use New Methods of Evangelizing

CONCLUSION

The Church began at Pentecost, when the Holy Spirit sent disciples, both men and women, out of a locked room and into a hostile world where they remembered and brought with them the lessons of Jesus, including his instructions on leadership and evangelization, which we have examined through the lens of the tenth chapter of Luke's gospel. We know that the disciples of Jesus were enormously successful because of that foundational training from Jesus himself. But the early disciples also remembered what Jesus had left them on the evening before his Passion, Death, and Resurrection. They had celebrated with him a sacred meal that they soon would come to call "Eucharist." Why did Jesus give us the Eucharist?

Our Lord knew that no motivational message lasts for long. Every great cause can fade, and this was a likely outcome for his disciples, who were going into hostile towns and villages and eventually to distant lands. Their mission needed continual renewal, and so our Lord provided a weekly gathering of worship and sacred meal to bring them spiritual sustenance that would keep them going. Today, we call this event that our Lord designed for our continual renewal the Mass.

Why would he choose this event as something to be repeated every week, often every day? Remember that the kingdom of God is entirely about living in the reality of God's love for us, which leads to our love of one another and ourselves. So how does love actually happen? Remember, love happens through meaningful conversations about the things that really matter in people's lives. That kind of talk is what people find most compelling and what draws them closer together. This is how people fall in love as God designed, become best friends, and solidify parent-child bonds.

Yet people rarely engage in this intimate level of talking unless they intentionally make time for it. They need to set up meaningful time with each other, such as a Friday night date or a Sunday afternoon walk around the block.

Our Lord understands this need for a regular time for meaningful talk about the larger context of your life and so asks you to meet and be in tune with him each Sunday. At Mass you will encounter your life with our Lord in terms of your eternal life, the largest context of all! You will encounter Jesus Christ's plan for how you can live the rest of your life in the most meaningful way—a way that provides for your lasting happiness. Just as God designed, this is where you will find your strength as a parish leader every week.

Along with encountering Christ in the Word proclaimed in the readings at Mass, in the prayers you utter aloud, and in the silences of the liturgy, you encounter Christ in the physical reality of the eucharistic bread and wine that become the Body and Blood of Christ. By eating and drinking what is set before you in the Eucharist, you are strengthened in your love for Christ and neighbor. Love changes everything! This love is where you will find the spiritual energy for your ministry, the courage for your leadership, and the happiness that makes it all meaningful and rewarding.

THE MASS ECHOES LUKE 10

Because the Mass itself echoes the principles of Luke 10 Leadership, participating in it reinforces your leadership training.

Christ first says peace in the opening greeting. In the penitential rite, he asks you to examine your personal culture and how you have perhaps done things not in accord with the kingdom of God. You examine what has nourished you recently that has been a problem. Next, he offers the cure of healing instruction through both scripture and a helpful homily. He then invites you to offer yourself in the offertory to be transformed at the consecration. You offer bread and wine, your entire self, and even your financial gifts for the good of the parish community. In the consecration, Jesus says the words that are the foundation of your life as a minister; he says, in essence, "This is my Body and Blood, my entire self, everything that I am and that I have received from my Father in heaven, and I offer it to you for your lasting happiness." No message could say more than that! Finally, you receive Christ into your body so that you become like him in your loving and then go into the world working to make the kingdom of God happen. Just as you have been personally transformed, you go out to transform the world.

A parishioner once told me she was concerned that during the meditation time after Communion, she was often distracted by thoughts of after-Mass events like shopping, visiting friends, and family activities. I told her these worldly events were *precisely* what she should be thinking about—but specifically about how she will be *different* at all these future events thanks to the presence of the Lord now within her because of the Eucharist! We do not leave our lives behind to commune with our Lord; rather, he came to Bethlehem to be with us in our everyday lives (see Philippians 2:6–11). Meeting Jesus makes every good thing happen and ushers in the kingdom of God.

This book has been about understanding and applying the training that Jesus gave his disciples in Luke 10 to bring about the kingdom of God. We end by understanding what our Lord intends for you now—that you will find your mission in the Mass, which ends with words that send you out to bring the kingdom of God courageously to a sometimes-hostile world, knowing he is always with you: "Go and announce the Gospel of the Lord!"

REV. DAVE HENEY is pastor of St. Bruno Catholic Church in Whittier, California, and the host of *The Family Rosary Across America* on Relevant Radio. Heney is the founder and director of The University Series, a Lenten, multi-parish adult education program that connects faith with real life, in the Archdiocese of Los Angeles.

Heney earned his bachelor's degree in existential philosophy (1974) and his master's of divinity degree (1978) from St. John's Seminary College. He was ordained a priest in the Archdiocese of Los Angeles in 1978. He earned his master of science degree in marriage, family, and child counseling from the University of Southern California at Los Angeles in 1991.

Heney is a chaplain of Legatus and leads annual archeological pilgrimages to the Holy Land. He is a member of the Equestrian Order of the Holy Sepulchre in Jerusalem, an international Vatican charity. Heney is the author of *Motivating Your Parish to Change* and *Don't Tell Me What to Do!: A Catholic Understanding of Modern Moral Issues*.

AVE

AVE MARIA PRESS

Founded in 1865, Ave Maria Press,
a ministry of the Congregation of
Holy Cross, is a Catholic publishing
company that serves the spiritual and
formative needs of the Church and its
schools, institutions, and ministers;
Christian individuals and families; and
others seeking spiritual nourishment.

For a complete listing of titles from

Ave Maria Press

Sorin Books

Forest of Peace

Christian Classics

visit www.avemariapress.com

AVE MARIA PRESS
Notre Dame, IN
A Ministry of the United States Province of Holy Cross